All On My Own

Sarah Dromey

authorHOUSE®

AuthorHouse™
1663 Liberty Drive
Bloomington, IN 47403
www.authorhouse.com
Phone: 1-800-839-8640

Published by AuthorHouse 12/03/2012

ISBN: 978-1-4772-4981-9 (sc)
ISBN: 978-1-4772-4982-6 (hc)
ISBN: 978-1-4772-4983-3 (e)

For my Dad who died from a stroke.

Contents

Introduction

One nice sunny evening in May 2010, I was early for salsa dancing in Turk's Head pub in Dublin city centre. I was sitting at the bar with a glass of water and I was dressed in my little green dress that I used to wear every Tuesday for salsa.

I must have been looking a bit depressed because a middle-aged man, probably in his fifties, came up to me and started talking to me. "What's wrong?" he said to me, "You have a beautiful figure". First of all, when I told him what age I was he couldn't believe it but sure no one does these days, so how could I expect him to be any different. We talked on a bit and he said to me again, "What's wrong". I said, "The man I love, I don't know where he is". We talked on, and I said to him, "I haven't slept with anyone". He said, "I can see that". We talked some more and then he said to me, "Have you even kissed this man?" I said, "No . . . I've danced with him". He said, "You've danced with him. Do you know something? That is the most romantic love story I've ever heard". Then I told him, "I only ever wanted one man". He said, "That's something I've been dreaming of my whole life". I told this man that it was time for me to go dancing. He said to me, "Don't worry about it, it's his loss" Then he gave me lots of kisses on my hand.

I've had a miserable past—a very hard life—which I always loved sharing with people because it helped to ease the weight on my shoulders, but I never knew where it was going. Now I have a romantic story to end it off with, and I want to share it with you.

September 2010, two weeks after my thirty-second birthday, and I was back in hospital. Alex McCarthy, what had he done to me? Now I was stuck in hospital all on my own and all I could think about was Alex. I didn't even have my mobile phone so I was really trapped there in that horrible ward in Tallaght Hospital. The first week I was hardly with it at all. I was very sick as I'd gone off my food and stopped my medication. Alex and myself had started a relationship in such a special and romantic way. Now it looked like he wanted more than a dance and I wasn't ready for that. I was still wearing a brace on my teeth, and there was no way I wanted to lose my virginity with a brace on. If we were going to make our relationship even more special than it already was, I had to get that brace off first.

I had the pill sorted, as I'd gone to the doctor about it before my head got messed up and I ended up in hospital. My next appointment with the orthodontist was in about two weeks, and I was pretty sure that I'd be getting it taken off then. My head was in a mess. All I could focus on was Alex. What was he doing? Was he wondering where I was? Alex was deep inside my heart. Even though I was alone in the hospital, just remembering all the times he'd touched my heart made me so happy. I had Alex inside me, so things weren't as bad as you might think.

My dad, Anthony Dromey, was born in a lovely town in Co. Waterford called Dungarvan. He had three older brothers and two younger brothers and he was squashed between his two sisters in the middle. My grandmother, who unfortunately I never met, died from a heart attack when my dad was only sixteen and my grandfather, who I never met either, was left to finish rearing his eight children on his own. After a few years, my grandfather met a lovely widow whose name was Lily. Lily had four children that she was raising on her own. They fell in love and got married. Now they were a family of fourteen. They were only married four years when my grandfather died from a stroke. Something that I feel is quite special in this family is that one of *his* children fell in love with one of *hers*. My dad's youngest brother fell in love with one of Lily's daughters and they got married. This created quite a bond between the two families.

Dad's eldest brother became a priest, and the rest of his siblings got married to lovely men and women, so the family grew even bigger. Before I was born, I already had six cousins on my dad's side and seven on my mother's side. My cousins, and my aunts and uncles, ended up being a big part of my life and I don't know what I would have done without them.

My dad was the last one to get married. He had gone travelling around Europe, and he'd also considered becoming a priest, but that didn't work out right for him. My dad met my mother when he was hill-walking one day. My mother had been travelling in the past too. She was a French teacher, and she'd been to France and loved it. She'd also spent three years in Zambia teaching. Given that they both loved travelling so much, it was kind of strange that we didn't travel abroad that much as a family while I was growing up.

Anyway, my parents met and, after a time, they ended up getting married. My mother put her eye on a five-bedroom house in Dublin and when my dad saw it he said,

"If you want this house you'll have to keep working".

My mother agreed and they bought the house. This house became the anchor in my life . . . the place where I felt loved, cared for, and happy. I only wish I wasn't taken away from it so often.

Not long after Mum and Dad moved into their new house my mother became pregnant with me. While she was in labour in the Coombe hospital in Dublin, I went into foetal distress and had to be delivered by forceps. A couple of years later, it was discovered that, as a result of this, I had epilepsy. Because of this, I spent the first twenty-six years of my life hoping and hoping for something I thought was never going to happen. It was like I was travelling down a long dark tunnel and I was pretty sure there was no light at the end of it. I had a great family and a great extended family, but I had no real friends for years, and nobody seemed to want to know who I was. *I* didn't even want to know who I was. As the years went on, my life just seemed to get worse, and there didn't seem much point in wanting anything in life because I never seemed to be able to get anything I wanted, or if I did, it was quite rare.

I had my first seizure when I was two years of age, and I can still remember the dark ambulance and the two or three men looking down at me. This is my first memory, and it's not a very pleasant one. One of my happiest memories is when I was about two or three and I was in the bath with my dad. I loved sitting down at the bottom of the bath with lovely warm water up to my neck and loads of bubbles. Normally I would have been given my bath in far less water, but my dad had put more water in the bath for himself, and his weight would have made the water rise up as well.

Both of my parents were working, so they had to find somebody to look after me. My lovely aunt Julie, on my dad's side of the family, took care of me when I was very small. Julie and my uncle Richard had a son called Richard, who was nine months younger than me. My mother tells this story that Julie told her. One day, while Julie was pushing the double buggy with Richard and myself in it, a woman came up to her and said,

"Are they twins?"

Julie replied, "No, there's nine months between them."

The woman gave Julie a strange look, but didn't say anything.

When I was just gone two years of age, Mum became pregnant again. When my parents were thinking of names for me, they'd decided on Sarah for a girl, and Peter for a boy. Nine months later, Mum went into labour again and had a lovely baby boy. My grandparents were looking after me while Mum was in hospital giving birth, and when my dad came home my grandmother asked him,

"What are you going to call him?"

When my dad said "Peter", my grandmother said

"Ah, I knew it was going to be either Peter or Paul, because today is the feast of Saint Peter and Paul. My parents didn't know that. What a coincidence. Dad just smiled.

I didn't have many toys when I was growing up. Now I had a lovely little baby brother, and I also had my mother with me for a few weeks. I always valued my time with her so much, as she was away from me a lot, working. I can remember Mum showing me how to change a nappy when I was only two or three years old, so I was introduced to taking care of babies very early in life. After that a doll was never good enough for me. I always longed to see what it was like to change a real baby's nappy, but like a lot of things in my life, I didn't tell anyone, I just kept it to myself.

Now there were two of us to be taken care of, so Mum and Dad had to find a minder for us. We ended up going to a kind of nursery a couple of miles away. The lady who ran the nursery was called Mrs. Jones. It wouldn't have been at all like the crèches these days. There would have been way less toys and far less children. I can remember really missing my little baby brother a lot while I was there, so I used to sneak out of the room to look into the room with all the cots where Peter was. I don't remember going outside at all, but I remember one thing very clearly, and that was that I learned how to tie my laces while I was there. I was so proud that I was able to tie my laces before my friend next door was able to.

For my fourth birthday I got a rust coloured bike with stabilisers. I rarely got anything that was pink. The one memory of something I got that was pink was a lovely little dress. I was only two or three at the time, and my mother was bringing me out to her school in Clontarf to show me to the other members of staff. I inherited travel sickness from my mother and got sick in the car on the way, so she had to buy me a new dress. I loved that dress so much I can still picture it.

My uncle James, on my mum's side of the family, was a paediatrician, and he gave Mum and Dad a kind of syrup medicine for my epilepsy. I remember being outside running around with the other children on the road and my dad coming out to give me a spoon of it. I'd run over to him, take it and then run back to the other children again. I remember one day one of the little boys saying to me,

"What's that?"

I answered, "I don't know but it's nice."

My epilepsy wasn't affecting my life too badly at that stage, but the worst was yet to come.

Christmas was always my favourite time of year when I was growing up. Not because of the presents, but because of the contact with family and friends. My cousins were my closest friends and I had fabulous neighbours too. Certain neighbours became a big part of my life as well, not so much as friends, but as very loving people who were always there for me. There were lots of other children living in the estate as well. I probably didn't talk to them that much because I was so shy and had no confidence, but I was very happy just to be in their company.

For me, Christmas always started on Christmas Eve. On the morning of Christmas Eve, I got the thrill of getting on the 15B bus into town. I got to go upstairs and over to the very front window on the top of the bus. That was a huge thing for me, because we rarely ever got the bus, we would have been driven everywhere. We went to Stephen's Green, and to Bewleys on Grafton Street. I got to see Santa in Switzers, and we got to see the magnificent Brown Thomas window. I remember going to see the Santas in the shops, and I always knew that it was just someone dressed up. I knew that it wasn't the Santa who left presents at the bottom of my bed. It wasn't the REAL Santa. I remember saying to my dad several years later,

"That's not the real Santa."

My dad said, "Why?"

I didn't answer him. I didn't know what to say.

Every year, my aunt Marie, (Dad's younger sister), gave a Christmas Eve party for all of the Dromeys over in her house, which wasn't too far away from us at all. There was always lots of lovely stuff to eat and drink, but the nicest and most important thing for me was being with family. The Christmas atmosphere was fantastic, and I got to run around and play with my cousins for a few hours. I always remember being sad when it was time for Richard to go home. They always seemed to be the first ones to leave. By the time we got home, it was time to put out the food for Santa and for Rudolph. Santa got a little glass of whiskey and some Christmas cake. Rudolph got a carrot, and I think he got Weetabix as well. Then we had to go to bed and try and relax and go to sleep, although of course we were all excited with Santa on his way.

After waking up early on Christmas morning, and getting a great thrill from seeing what Santa had left for us, we'd go to 8 o'clock mass. Dad used to get a bit claustrophobic with crowds of people in the church, so we went to the early Mass because there were very few people at it. After Mass, we'd go home and have a big fry-up for breakfast, and then we'd go over to Richard and Julie's house. We'd get to play with little Richard and then in later years with Aidan, who was born when I was about six.

Once we got home, Mum's attention would be focused on preparing the big Christmas dinner. My grandparents would come over sometime between twelve and one with Christmas presents. There were very few Christmases when I actually liked the presents I got from my grandparents, but I'd just smile and say thank you. One year I got a jumper that my grandma had knitted for me and I remember being quite disappointed. As the years went by, it turned out that I actually got more enjoyment from opening up the presents and hoping I'd like them, rather than from the presents themselves. I can remember one Christmas early on in life when my godmother came over with a selection box, and I was delighted, but I don't remember getting any selection boxes after that.

One of the things I loved most about Christmas was decorating the house, and I got more into it as I got older. Dad used to make the crib with a cardboard box and hard black paper. When I was small I didn't like this at all. I used to say to him,

"I thought Jesus was born in a stable?"

Dad said, "It could have been a cave either."

I loved the holly, and when I was small I remember wanting a fake tree, because I'd seen them in other people's houses, but Dad wasn't having it. When he didn't let me have what I wanted, he still wouldn't say "No". Mum would say "No" without giving a reason, and I hated that, but Dad would say something like,

"We don't have to be like everyone else." He rarely said "No".

[illegible] Christmas [illegible] when [illegible] came [illegible] with a [illegible] and [illegible] [illegible]

[illegible]

One of the [illegible] Christmas [illegible] and black paper [illegible]

I thought Jesus was born in a stable?"

Dad said, "It could [illegible]"

[illegible] the holy [illegible] all the [illegible] because [illegible] other people [illegible] When [illegible] Mommy [illegible] said [illegible] but Dad would say something like

"We don't have to be like everyone else, [illegible]," said [illegible]

Chapter 3

I started school when I was five, and my little brother Peter was two now, so it was time to get another minder. My parents decided on a woman called Betty, aged about twenty-nine and from Tallaght, to look after Peter in the mornings, and the two of us when I got home from school, while they were at work. Looking back on it, I don't think she liked me very much. I think she took to Peter more. She used to love sitting in the rocking chair in front of the television, watching all the soaps. She used to watch snooker too, and although I'm sure she never realised, it helped Peter a lot with his maths and colours. He also developed a love of snooker.

At this time in my life, I had a best friend called Aisling, who was about three months older than me. She lived next door and we spent a lot of time together. I used to go and see her after school, when I'd finished eating the horrible honey sandwiches, made with *brown* bread, which seemed to be the standard lunch menu. I hated brown bread at the time. I'd ask for white bread but I was told 'brown bread is better for you'. I'd be sitting at the kitchen table and I'd shout into Betty,

"I don't like them."

Betty would shout back at me, from her seat in front of the television,

"EAT THEM!!"

One day I came home from school to find ketchup sandwiches waiting for me. It was such a pleasant surprise that I actually finished my lunch before Aisling was finished eating hers. I often remember standing at the back door of Aisling's house, and watching her trying to eat a lovely big plate of mashed potato with cabbage mashed into it. Aisling would shout into her mother,

"Just three more spoonfuls."

I'd be thinking to myself, just give it to me, and I'll finish it in no time, but I was too quiet and well behaved. I tended to keep my thoughts and feelings to myself.

Anytime I'd call "Betty", for any reason whatever, Betty would reply "What!!", while she sat in the rocking chair, glued to the soaps on the television. She had very little time for Peter or myself at all. So I ended up getting into the habit of replying "What", to people. Aisling's mother, Ruth, said to me one time,

"It's not what Sarah, it's yes."

She also encouraged me to answer "Hi" back to her when she said "Hi Sarah" to me. I was always so shy. In a way it was like Ruth was looking after me more than Betty was. I remember standing in her kitchen watching her wash Aisling's hair, and standing in their bathroom upstairs while Aisling and her cousin Rebecca had a bath together. I felt much more at home, and safe, in their company than in Betty's. I don't think Betty was that loving a person at all. Not in my book anyway.

My Dad kept bees as a hobby, so we always had loads of honey in the house. His grandfather was a beekeeper too. I'd say the cupboards were empty enough apart from that. Mum was so busy teaching that she never bought anything that wasn't necessary, and she probably didn't have the money anyway. She did one shop on a Thursday, and just got the necessities to last us the week. When I'd go shopping with Mum, it seemed like anything I asked her for, she always answered "No", so I just ended up following her miserably around the shop. I hated the way Peter got to sit in the trolley and I had to walk. There was one time, I think it was in Wexford, when we all went shopping together, and my dad was pushing the trolley. I asked him if I could sit in it, thinking there was no chance, but Dad just lifted me up and put me in the trolley. I couldn't believe it, I was delighted.

I didn't like washing my hands very much, but I have a really nice memory of my mum washing my hands in the sink after I'd been to the toilet. She covered her own hands in soap first, and then I reached my hands up and put them under the running water, and Mum rubbed her soapy hands all around mine. It was lovely.

I hated visiting my grandparents when I was small. It was always so boring, although I do remember that my grandpa used to hide mini Mars bars for Peter and myself to find. I'd always end up seeing one as soon as I came out of the kitchen, but for some reason, I always let Peter find his first. I never really liked them that much anyway. One time I was in the kitchen with my grandpa and I said "No" to something he said.

My grandpa replied, "No is a horrible word."

This must have made a big impression on me, because even now, at the age of thirty-two, I still find it very difficult to say "No" to somebody, though I have to say Alex is helping me there without knowing it. In this world you have to be able to say "No". Alex has no problem at all saying "No", and I actually find the way he said "NO" to me hilarious. He said it so suddenly, so sharply, and even kind of defensively.

I hated learning my table manners, and thinking about it brings back bad memories of my mum. Learning how to hold my knife and fork wasn't too bad but the thing I hated was the elbows.

"Sarah, take your elbows off the table," my mum would say.

"But Dad has his elbows on the table," I would reply.

"Well, Dad is Dad".

I felt it wasn't fair that Dad could put his elbows on the table and we couldn't. Anyway I did what I was told. Whenever we had chicken for dinner, we'd have great fun pulling the wishbone, and we always wished for the same thing every time . . . a nice place in the country where Dad could keep his bees.

When Peter was about two and I was about five, Mum got very sick. She got a blockage in one of her fallopian tubes, and the doctor thought it might have been an ectopic pregnancy. Mum was advised to stay in bed to see if the blockage would move. She ended up losing loads of weight, but the blockage never moved, and in the end, she had to go into hospital and have surgery. When they opened her up, they discovered that she had an ovarian cyst as well. They removed the ovary that had the cyst, and had to cut the fallopian tube to the other ovary. This meant that Mum couldn't have any more children. I was very disappointed when I heard this because I really wanted another brother or sister. After that, I always wanted a dog as another companion in life. I think Dad would have loved a dog as well, but Mum wasn't having one.

Dad used to go out playing golf with his brothers at the weekend, and when I'd say to Mum,

"Where's Dad?" she'd just say, "He'll be back later."

My Dad loved us so much that when he heard how much I missed him while he was gone, he stopped playing golf. He still kept very fit though. Mum and Dad just had one car like most families at that time. Dad used to cycle to work so that Mum could take the car to school. He used to cycle six miles there and six miles home every day, except Saturday and Sunday of course. He also used to go for walks by himself in the evening when it was dark. He'd wear his overcoat, and a lovely hat he had with a little feather in the side of it. At the time, I couldn't understand how anyone could enjoy walking on their own in the dark, although now I love walking by myself or with others—it's all the same to me. Sometimes walking by myself is more enjoyable, because I like to walk at quite a fast pace, and if you're walking with someone else they might slow you down.

One summer we went camping in a place called Clonbur in county Mayo, when I was about four or five. We had two tents, one for sleeping in and another for anything else we needed it for. We camped by Lough Mask, and I remember all the rowing boats along the side of the lake. Dad used to go out fishing with my mum's uncle, Tom. I didn't like the look of Tom at all. He always looked so miserable. That's because he had a hard life but we won't go into that. I don't think I liked camping that much. It was kind of exciting putting up the tents, but after that it got quite boring. Sometimes, though, Dad might take Peter and myself out in the little rowing boat, and he'd give me a go at rowing, but of course I could never manage it. We used to do a bit of fishing with him as well, but we'd never catch anything.

Chapter 4

When I started school the big thing was, who was going to be in my class. Aisling was a year ahead of me so I knew she'd be in a different class. As it happened, there were three boys in my class that I knew from Mrs. Jones's . . . Steve, Peter, and Liam. There was another boy called Adam, who was a friend of Steve's, and they both lived around the corner from me. I think I latched on to them pretty quickly, and Steve in particular. I took a shine to Steve, and Adam took a shine to me, although I never actually realised it, as I was so into Steve. My teacher's name was Miss Watson. I remember the 'Ann and Barry' book when I was starting to learn to read. I think I wrote Ann and Barry on the wallpaper in the hall at home, or maybe that was Peter a few years later. Either way, Mum had to live with 'Ann and Barry' on her wallpaper for years, as my parents couldn't afford to do up the house. When I first started school, I remember Dad standing by the wall in the classroom, because I didn't want to be left on my own. I was a very shy child, very insecure and not good at mixing with anyone. Although I remember Steve saying to me in junior infants,

"Let's get married."

When I said "We can't," Steve said,

"Why not"?

I said, "We're too young." He totally lost interest after that. I didn't though. I kept chasing him for a long time.

At the end of the year in junior infants, I remember being very disappointed because I couldn't go on the school tour to the zoo. Mum and Dad were taking us to France instead. I'd never been to the zoo, because Dad didn't like the idea of animals being locked up in cages. The trip to France wasn't much fun at all, starting with the ferry. While Dad was going all around the ferry with Peter, Mum and myself were stuck in the cabin, seasick. I got the top bunk, which was nice, but apart from that it was torture . . . sick in bed all the way from Rosslare to Le Havre. Mum and Dad had rented a gite to the south of Brittany, but as they couldn't find a place that was available for two weeks running, they ended up having to rent two different gites.

The first week was okay. I relate it to the colour green for some reason. It was a house on a farm and there were two other children there for a few of the days, so it wasn't so bad. There were loads of rabbits in cages, and I remember trying to feed them hay, but they wouldn't really eat it. Of course we were never told that they were going to be killed and cooked for dinner somewhere. There were swings and a see-saw there as well, and towards the end of the week, the farmer gave Peter and myself a ride on his tractor, which was quite exciting.

The second week was horrible. I associate this week with the colour brown. There were no children to be seen, in fact I don't think there was really anyone else around at all. It was really boring, and I couldn't stop thinking about the fact that I could have been at the zoo.

I had Miss Watson as my teacher again in senior infants. The one thing that really sticks in my mind about that year is that getting up for school was such a chore. Mum would come into my bedroom and basically had to pull me out of bed. She'd get me dressed and bring me downstairs for breakfast . . . Weetabix, which I didn't like at the time. Then I'd be taken to school either by Mum, on her way to work, or by one of Aisling's parents, usually her dad. I used to walk home from school with Betty, but I'm not sure whether Peter was with us. She always took the same way home, but I wanted to walk a different way, a way that I thought would have been quicker but Betty just said,

"NO, this way's quicker."

Looking at it now, I'd say they're pretty similar, but my way might have been slightly quicker. Of course there was no chance of Betty carrying my school-bag either. Maybe she just preferred listening to me say how heavy it was.

Around this time, I got chickenpox for the second time. Seemingly I got a mild dose as a baby, but this time it was a really bad dose. I had them on my tongue and all. I remember looking at the first one while I was with Aisling. It was so painful trying to resist the itch, and I was nearly crying because of it. Aisling's mother, Ruth, told me just after I got it, that she'd get me something nice if I didn't scratch my body. I wanted to be with Aisling, but of course I couldn't, because she could catch the chickenpox from me. I remember Dad saying,

"She's going to get it anyway."

Sure enough, Aisling had it a few weeks later. Of course I was able to see her and spend time with her then, because I was immune at that stage.

When I was better, Ruth bought me a book. I never liked getting a present of a book because I was really bad at reading. I just couldn't take in the words. I couldn't picture them in my head. But I loved looking at the pictures. This was a very good book though. It had a short version of the story on one side of the book in big letters, and a longer version of the story in smaller letters on the opposite page. I remember the big print on the left and the small print on the right. There were nice pictures as well.

Even though Mum and Dad were big readers themselves, they never read to us that much. Mum used to read to us when she was putting us to bed, but she was wrecked after her day at work, and it was obvious that reading the story was a real chore for her. I always got the impression that she was dying to get the book finished, and over and done with. This wasn't helpful for me in terms of my attitude towards reading. I found it hard enough to read as it was. But one time Dad read to us, and he put such great expression into his voice that I thought it was amazing, but that was the only time I can remember him reading to us.

When Aisling was better, my mum bought her an advent calendar, so I suppose I must have got the chickenpox sometime in November.

There was one game in particular that I liked playing with Aisling . . . hopscotch. You'll notice that the games I enjoyed playing most with the children on the road were games that didn't involve much conversation or communication. On one of Aisling's birthday parties, her parents bought her a Hansel and Gretel birthday cake. I thought it was brilliant, and when my birthday was coming up, I kept asking my mum to buy me a Hansel and Gretel cake as well. She said "No", and then she said,

"I'll make you a Hansel and Gretel cake myself." I was very satisfied with this arrangement, because Mum is brilliant at baking. She made me a fabulous cake with chocolate finger biscuits for the roof, and Liquorice Allsorts for the windows and the door. I was so proud of that cake. It was one of the best things my mum ever did for me.

When I look back on my birthdays, the part of the day that I enjoyed the most was the time before the other children came, when Mum was making all the buns, and chocolate squares, and all the other sweet things for the party, and of course the birthday cake as well. I was such a shy and quiet child that once the other children came, it wasn't so much fun at all. I didn't get as much attention then, and all the children would be playing with each other, and I'd be left all on my own for a lot of it. I enjoyed opening the presents, and I joined in with some of the games, but I never enjoyed it as much as the preparation for the party.

One morning when Aisling's dad was driving the two of us up to school, Aisling said to him

"Will I tell her?"

Her dad said "Yes."

Aisling told me they were going away for two years. This came as a huge shock to me. Aisling's dad was in the army, his work was taking him to the Middle East for two years, and he was taking his family with him. I couldn't believe it. I was totally devastated. I didn't say anything. I just kept it to myself and dealt with it all by myself. My best friend was leaving me for two years, and I didn't really have any other friends. Two years is long enough for an adult, but you can imagine how long it seems to a small child. For me, it seemed like an eternity.

Chapter 5

After a lot of searching around the country for a place to keep Dad's bees, Mum and Dad finally decided on a bungalow on three quarters of an acre of land in a place called Garryvadden. It was an old, and very small townland, three miles from Blackwater village in Co. Wexford.

I remember the first time Dad took us to see it. The house was plonked in the middle of a field that was full of small holes everywhere. The family who owned it before us had built the house themselves, and had been keeping their sheep on the land, which was uneven and needed to be levelled out. There was a red, rusty copper gate like one you'd see when you were looking into a field with cows in it. Across from the bungalow, there was a big red barn with a lot of land around it to the left and the right. I discovered later that this land on both sides ran down to a small river. There were no roads to be seen anywhere, just lots of fields that you got to off a very small lane with grass growing in the middle. It was always really quiet and peaceful which was great for Mum and Dad, because they were delighted to get away from the fast pace of Dublin and all the pressure that came with it.

There were very few houses to be seen and not a child in sight. I remember dreaming that if I had a dog, the two of us could go running up the field together, but unfortunately that dream never came true. The journey from Dublin to Garryvadden took us two hours. I ended up lying down on the back seat for most of the journey, and probably sleeping most of it as well, because I got travel sickness every time. The journey down always seemed like such a chore, and I hated it. It was bad enough being taken away from our life in Dublin, but to have to spend two hours sick in the back of the car as well made it so much worse. I'd have to go through it on Sundays as well on the way back to Dublin. Peter would have been annoying me as well. He was either pulling my plaits or we'd just be fighting over the space in the back of the car.

"Get back, you're on my side".

One time I got so mad with Peter pulling my plaits that I felt like biting him, but I guess I was just too nice a sister to go through with the idea. I couldn't bear the idea of hurting Peter.

One time we went down there, Mum and Dad couldn't get the car into the field, because the tyres kept slipping on the muddy hill. So I think the first improvement Dad made to his new property was to get gravel down to make a driveway up the hill and around the front of the house, and the left side of the house as you looked at it from the front.

When Mum and Dad got the place first all the windows were boarded up, so that all had to be removed. Every Friday evening when we arrived down, the routine was that the first thing Dad would do was go into the sitting room and light a fire to warm up the house. There was no proper heating system, and the house was very badly insulated, so it would always take ages to heat up. Anyway, I'd always go into the fireplace with my dad and watch him light the fire. He showed me how to light a fire using newspaper and twigs. I became very good at lighting fires and after a few years, this became my job. While Dad was lighting the fire with me beside him, Mum would be taking care of the beds. I'm not sure what the sleeping arrangements were when we got the place first. I have a feeling it was like camping, so I don't think there were any beds at all. I think we slept on air beds in sleeping bags. Mum and Dad were given second-hand beds from each of Dad's sisters. The double bed was from Rose, and the single bed was from Marie. Rose also gave Mum and Dad some carpet she was finished with, and they laid it in the sitting room. In the spring and autumn, Mum would have put electric blankets on the beds as well. The house was so cold it's amazing that we actually managed to heat it up at all.

At first, the only things in the kitchen were a poky little sink in the corner, and a Rayburn that backed onto the fireplace in the sitting room, as they both shared the chimney. The Rayburn was cream coloured, and it had a main oven, that showed the temperature on the outside, and a lower oven. The right-hand side was the section where the fire was, and another door below it for the ashes. On the Friday night, after Dad had got a good fire going in the sitting room, he'd transfer a good chunk of the fire into the Rayburn, and then on the Saturday morning the kitchen would be lovely and warm. The odd Saturday morning, Mum would make scones, and it was lovely to wake up to the fabulous smell of freshly made scones, and go into a lovely warm kitchen to eat them.

Rose also gave us a table for the kitchen, and we got furniture from my uncle Martin, my dad's second youngest brother too. In the sitting room, we had a few tables that my grandpa had made himself. Sometimes, during the year, there'd be a furniture sale in Blackwater village and we'd all go into it. Mum and Dad got some great bargains there. In particular, I remember the wardrobes, and a couch and chairs.

The bathroom in the house was pretty basic, just a bath that would have been too small for Dad, a sink and a toilet. We had awful trouble with the toilet, which had the weirdest flush button I'd ever seen. There wasn't a handle on the side like most toilets. Instead, there was a thing like a big cylinder on top of the cistern in the middle, and you had to push it down to flush the toilet. I don't think there was hot water in the bathroom either. After a good few years we got the bathroom fixed up a bit with a new toilet and hot water, and Dad did a lot of the plumbing himself. The best thing was that we got an electric shower put in, which made things a lot better.

My next year in school was first class and I had a new teacher, Mrs. Mitchell. I hated her . . . she was so mean to me. I remember learning to bless myself. Religion was very important this year, as I was going to be making my first Holy Communion. All through this time, I had a big dark shadow haunting me. That's what happened every time I had a seizure. I never really knew what was happening to me, but all of a sudden, this horrible feeling would start coming over me, and I knew I was going to be taken away from life as I knew it, and that I was going to be swallowed up into a living nightmare that wouldn't leave me alone. You could say it was like an out-of-body experience. It was horrible, and it prevented me from doing all the things that the other children could do, swimming for instance. There was one day in the school week when we could go to the pool and learn how to swim. Mum and Dad made the mistake of letting me go swimming with the class. Seemingly, I wanted to go swimming so much that they couldn't keep me from it, and they let me go with the class.

One day I had a seizure in the pool. I never really realised this for years, but I can still remember Mrs. Mitchell pulling my pinafore over my head so forcefully when I was only half with it. It was horrible, and I didn't know what was going on. But I remember Adam, the boy who lived around the corner and who had a crush on me, saying to me,

"I dived in and saved you."

I didn't know what he was going on about at the time, but looking back on it, I can see that he must have seen the lifeguard diving into the pool and was trying to impress me. I can still picture myself sitting on a chair in the principal's office, watching him giving out to my parents for letting me go swimming.

I wasn't allowed to go swimming with the class anymore, and I had to stay behind with a handful of other children. The one good thing that came out of that whole episode was that it gave me a good reason to learn how to swim. After that, Mum and Dad used to take Peter and myself to Templeogue swimming pool on Sunday mornings, and that's where I learned to swim. After swimming, Mum and myself would go back into the changing room together, but for some reason, Mum wouldn't let me go into the shower. I think she just didn't see the point of it, but I wasn't happy about it, as Peter and Dad used to have great fun messing about in the shower, and Mum and myself were always waiting ages for the two of them to come out of the changing rooms. But of course I never said a thing. I never complained about it to Mum, probably because I knew it wouldn't get me anywhere, as I rarely got what I wanted, particularly from Mum.

Even though Peter and myself were always fighting over things, like most brothers and sisters, he always set a good example for me. After he had learned to swim with the school, Peter would be showing me what he could do and teaching me how to do it. This really helped my swimming. Then, when he was doing tennis with the school, I used to go along with him. I didn't take part in the classes, but I used to love just watching them learn how to play tennis, and I loved running around picking up the tennis balls, and bringing them back to the players.

Chapter 6

Now that Aisling was gone, I don't know what I did after school, apart from doing my homework and changing out of my school uniform. These were routines that I hated. I was so tired after walking down from school with a heavy bag on my back, that changing my clothes was a huge drag. I couldn't understand why a lot of the other children didn't have to change out of their uniforms, but I did. Anyway, I'd change when I got home, and then I was supposed to do my homework straight afterwards, and get it out of the way. That was the routine Mum had got us into.

When it came to my schoolwork, I wasn't confident at all with my ability to learn. I ended up waiting the hour until Mum came home, so I could get help from her, and that would give me the confidence to do my homework. What a waste of an hour, and it always took so long for me to get my homework done, even with Mum's help. I was very slow at writing for some reason, I really don't know why. Although it might have been because the medication I was on caused my hands to shake, and that would have slowed me down at writing.

I think Mrs. Mitchell took the swimming incident out on me by giving me extra work to take home. Anything I wasn't able to take down off the board, or finish in class, she would get me to do on top of my homework. My dad went up to Mrs. Mitchell quite a number of times asking her to go easy on me, but she was never nice to me. She was my worst teacher throughout all my education, and she always seemed to make life harder for me.

I had hardly any social life at all. It was just come home from school, wait for Mum to come home from school, do my homework and then go to bed. I remember kicking a football around with Steve and Adam around the corner, but again, even though I spent time with them, I did very little talking to them, so my social skills weren't developing very well at all.

We'd be in Dublin at the weekends from Halloween to Easter, when it was too cold to go down to Wexford. Saturday mornings were great. Peter and myself would go downstairs when we woke up, and watch all the children's programmes that were on the television. When we were in Wexford, we only had a tiny black and white television, and even worse we only had two channels, with a very bad quality picture on the little screen. I'm not sure what I did on Saturdays when I was in Dublin, but I would have spent a lot of time with my cousin Richard. He would have stayed overnight in our house and vice versa. There were times when I wanted to go to the park with Richard and his parents, but they tended to be busy a lot of Saturdays, so we ended up going on Sundays.

I really liked the park, and feeding the ducks and the swans was such a great thrill at that time of the year, when there were little ducklings and cygnets. I loved looking at the waterfall. It seemed magical to me as we walked up the steps beside it. Dad used to push us on the swings in the playground, and I'd be saying to him "higher, higher". There was a forest area in the park as well and I used to love exploring it with my Dad. I loved my Dad so much. He never said "No" to me, and he always did his best to make me happy.

On Sunday morning, the only thing on the television was Mass, and Peter and myself found it pretty boring. Mum used to take us to the ten o'clock Mass. It was a special children's mass where a group of children put on a little play of the gospel. I wanted to be an altar girl like some of the other children, but Mum wouldn't let me because of being away in Wexford so often. I remember learning to pray and I couldn't understand how Jesus could be the bread. It just looked like wafer to me. I hated kneeling down to pray because it hurt my thighs. I also hated closing my eyes while I was praying.

I couldn't see the point of it. After a while I'd kneel down all right, but I wouldn't bother closing my eyes. There was a lovely children's choir at this Mass as well, and of course I couldn't be part of that because I didn't have a note in my head. I probably wouldn't have been allowed because of Wexford anyway.

Sometimes I'd spend time with my cousins Caitriona and Siobhan, Auntie Marie's two girls, that's my Dads younger sister. Sometimes Caitriona and Siobhan would stay overnight with us, and other times Peter and myself would go over to their house and stay the night with them. One time, Auntie Marie, Caitriona and Siobhan cycled over to our house and I remember Siobhan trying to get me to sit on the back of her bike, but I felt I was too big to let her give me a ride on it. Then I sat on the back of Auntie Marie's bike as we cycled back over to their house, and I loved it. When Peter went over to stay with Caitriona and Siobhan he used to mess with their piano, and one time he broke one of the keys and Auntie Marie had to get it fixed.

When the teachers were preparing us for our Communion, the whole class went to the church together, and the children were being paired up to practise walking out of the oratory and up the aisle. I was paired with Adam first, and then the teacher changed her mind and paired me with Steve. I was a lot happier with this arrangement as I fancied Steve.

That was a thing with me though, when it came to the children having to line up and get into pairs. Because I had no friends, I usually ended up all on my own at the back of the line. I never really liked my Communion dress, it was third hand, Caitriona and Siobhan had worn it before me. Anyway the dress was too short on me, and I particularly hated the way the sleeves were too short. My brother Peter got a second-hand blazer but at least he got new trousers, a new tie, a lovely new shirt and of course new shoes. I just got new shoes and new knee-high socks to cover my bruised legs. All the other girls were so pretty in their new dresses. I didn't feel pretty at all.

Of course I never really felt pretty or beautiful as a child. I was a real tomboy, not very girlie at all. I'm sure I had the potential to be a beautiful little princess, which my parents would have always seen me as anyway, but no, I was a real tomboy, always wanting to do what the boys were doing, and especially what Peter was doing. I hated getting my hair washed, that was the worst. It always took so long for my hair to dry. I had a big mop of hair and I hated the way Peter didn't have to get conditioner. He had it over and done with in no time and was able to go out and play again. There was one time when Dad was cutting Peter's hair, and I decided I was sick of having long hair and I wanted my hair cut as well. So Dad cut my hair, and after that everyone thought I was a boy until I grew it long again.

It was around this time that I lost my first tooth. So I left my tooth under my pillow, and in the morning I found a pound note that the tooth fairy had left for me in exchange for my tooth. This was great. Not only did I have Santa there for me, but now I had the tooth fairy as well. Though I could never understand why I only got fifty pence for all of my other teeth, when I got a pound for my first tooth. If I were to give a child a reason for this now, it would be that there are a lot of different tooth fairies, and the one that left the pound note mustn't have been strong enough to carry fifty pence, so she gave you a pound note instead.

Another time of the year that I loved was the August bank holiday weekend. My dad's older sister Rose, who lives in Dungarvan, was the only one of all my dad's siblings who didn't move to Dublin. Rose and her husband Jack bought a lovely bungalow just up the road from the house that she, Dad and all their siblings grew up in. And although Dad's younger sister Marie and her husband live in Dublin, they also bought a lovely cottage near the old family home in Dungarvan. We used to stay for a few days a year with Rose and Jack, and play with our cousin Jack who's about ten years older than me. Jack used to give Peter and myself piggybacks, which was great fun altogether. They also owned a lovely pony called Muncher. Muncher was a very big pony, nearly the size of a horse, and I always thought of him as a beautiful white horse that we used to get to ride on every summer, and I remember giving him some apple after I was finished riding him. They had cats as well, and lovely little kittens, so it really was a lovely experience going down to Dungarvan every year.

One year, I'm not sure what age I was at the time, my aunt Marie started a tradition of a barbecue at their cottage in Dungarvan on the August bank holiday weekend. Most of my dad's siblings and their families would turn up and Lily, my dad's stepmother, and her children and their families would come as well. Everyone would bring their own meat and maybe other food to share as well. There was a good crowd of us, and I used to love playing with all my cousins and step-cousins as well. I have a vague memory of the four of us staying with Lily in Tipperary at one stage too. She owned a B&B there, and I used to play with her grandson Keith, who's about the same age as me. I thought it was amazing the way he was able to slide down the banisters.

One year while we were staying with Rose and Jack, I got very sick. I can still remember lying in the bed retching and complaining about pain in my tummy. After a while, Mum and Dad drove us back to Garryvadden. At some stage, Mum and Dad decided to try me with some ice cream, but I vomited it up. When Dad saw this he said,

"If she can't take ice cream then there must be something wrong."

So they took me to a doctor somewhere in Wexford.

The doctor put me up on the bed and tapped his fingers on my tummy. After about two or three times I said "Ow". The doctor immediately said,

"Appendix, into hospital straight away."

My parents considered bringing me up to Dublin, and they phoned my uncle who was a doctor for advice, but in the end, they decided on Wexford hospital. It's just as well they did, because very soon after I was brought in I was taken down for surgery. I was terrified when they wheeled me away from my parents and down a long narrow corridor. I was screaming and crying. I can still remember the doctors and nurses struggling trying to get the mask over my nose to put me to sleep. If they'd only let Mum or Dad come with me I would have been grand.

When I woke up I was in a ward with two or three other girls a bit younger than me. I looked down at my tummy and saw lots of blood. The nurses came and patched me up. As the days went by, I progressed to walking to the toilet with the nurse by my side. The toilet was a good distance away for a little girl with a very sore side. I remember the nurse saying to me,

"Stand up straight or you'll be bent over when you're older."

So I did my best to walk without bending over a bit, but it was really sore.

I got very upset one morning because my mum hadn't come into the hospital yet. Mum used to stay with me in the morning, and Dad would stay in the evening until I fell asleep. I hated being on my own. Anyway, this morning Mum was late coming in and I started to cry. I remember the nurse shouting out to me,

"Stop that crying."

The nurses weren't very nice at all in Wexford hospital at the time. I remember talking to my Dad about my tummy while I was in hospital. I was devastated that I'd have a scar for the rest of my life. I said to my Dad,

"Will it ever go away?"

Dad said, "The marks going across might fade but the main line will always be there."

Over the past number of years, a lot had happened in Garryvadden. Mum and Dad had become friends with an old couple who lived about half a mile up the road, Sean Walsh and his wife Mary, who was known to everyone as Minnie. They had a black retriever dog called Darky. Sean and Minnie lived in a little cottage on an acre of land. They had raised ten children in this cottage, which only had two rooms upstairs and two rooms downstairs. Most of the children had emigrated, and they never got in touch, as they were very annoyed at the way Sean had treated them and their mother as they were growing up. Minnie had it very hard. They had no running water, so she had to carry water about half a mile up the hill from the well across the road from us. Sean tells the story that one day he decided to dig a well. He had dug down about ten feet, and then Minnie called him for his tea. He climbed out, and when he came back out after his tea, the well had caved in. He could have been buried alive.

Down the hill a bit nearer to us lived Mrs. Kelly, and two of her children, Ned and Joan, who were middle aged. Ned ran the farm and Joan took care of the house. Their one other sibling, Ellen, got married and had thirteen children—ten girls and three boys, with one set of twins. The entrance to the farm was a big, green metal gate off Garryvadden lane, and it lead on to a small, dark muck lane with tall trees on either side. They had a dog named Shep, and they had hens pecking around the land behind the house, and there were old outhouses great for exploring, especially for Dubs who hadn't seen anything like it before.

Then there was Ian, Ian Kelly. He was what you might call different. He lived in a big house just up the lane from ours with his mother, who I don't know if I ever saw at all. Ian was left quite a big farm when his father died, but he was really a pretty bad farmer. He much preferred just messing about with old machinery, cars and tractors. You should have seen his back yard. It was full of junk, most of which was metal. Ian kept to himself most of the time. I don't think he was the easiest person to talk to, but he didn't cause any trouble and that was the main thing. I remember actually being scared of him, that's how peculiar he was.

We also became friends with Alex Kelly, who lived a bit further away from us. He owned the land across from us, and the big field up from us. The family who had owned his land and ours had divided it into two lots and sold them separately—the house on three quarters of an acre of the land to my parents, who used every penny they had to buy it, and the rest of their land which they sold to Alex Kelly. Alex had a lot of children as well. The three youngest, Collette, Joan and Charlie used to come over and play with us sometimes, which we loved, as most of the time it was just Peter and myself.

At one stage, Alex was growing turnips on half of the land he owned across from us. The well on his land was the one that Minnie, the woman with the ten children, used to get the water from. The running water we had in the house came from this well too, and Alex was very good to let us continue to use it, as it was on his land. The pump wasn't very good, and it caused a lot of problems so we had to contact Alex quite a bit. I think he was actually glad that we were there to tell him when it wasn't working, because it was the same pump that pumped the water up to the trough for the cattle.

Peter and myself went down with Dad to see the well. There was water running out of the side of it like a very small stream. There must have been a crack in the cement or something. There was loads of frog spawn, and a lot of watercress as well, which we found very interesting, and after a time the frog spawn turned to tadpoles. Peter and myself used to collect the tadpoles in jars and bring them back to the house. Of course the tadpoles always ended up dying and I don't know what we did with them when they did. We probably just emptied the contents of the jars onto the grass. There were frogs too, something you'd never see in Dublin. I can remember lifting them up and thinking it was great fun altogether.

Paddy and Eileen Murray lived down the hill a bit from Alex. They were lovely, and they had four children when we met them first, two boys and two girls. Over the years they had another girl. We used to go over to their house and play, and we had great fun with them. They owned a farm as well and it was mainly sheep that Paddy farmed. They had dogs too, but I can't remember their names. One time when we were over with them it was shearing time.

It was fascinating watching them shave the wool off the sheep, and in particular, the way they held the sheep while they were doing it. When they'd finished taking all the wool off, it was lovely to see the sheep walking away without a bother on them. They didn't mind what was being done to them at all.

Another time when we were over with them it was dipping time. It was great watching the sheep being guided into the water and being moved along through it, having their heads pushed under the water for a second, and then seeing the sheep coming happily up the steps at the end.

Early on when we met Paddy for the first time, Dad agreed with him that they'd plant a load of potatoes up in the top half of our land. I don't remember Paddy ploughing the land or planting the potatoes, but I can remember the big group of us that helped collect up all the potatoes when they were ready. All the potatoes were stored in one of the rooms in our house, the room with the cement floor that we didn't use for anything. I can remember going through the potatoes with Mum and sorting them out into good ones, and ones that had gone off. I didn't particularly enjoy doing this but there probably wasn't anything else for me to do anyway.

There was an old man whose name was Fred O'Neill. He lived in a little old house with a corrugated roof, off the side of Garryvadden lane. I'd say the house had two rooms at the most. It looked very small anyway, and I couldn't see any windows. Fred was an only child, and we used to bump into him sometimes in the evening when we were walking to the triangle. About a mile down the hill from our house there was a T junction, and in the middle of the road was a grass triangle. It was a lovely walk down to it, and if we met Fred we'd usually end up chatting for quite a while as the sun went down. Fred was lovely, I really liked him. He was very contented living in his little house on the side of the lane by himself, with no dog or anything.

Paddy introduced us to a man called Ian Murray, but although they had the same surname, they weren't related. Ian was married to Linda and they had one daughter called Denise. Ian was a builder, but he kept some sheep as well. Basically, he did a bit of this and a bit of that . . . Dad needed someone like Ian to do some work on our land and to fix it up the house a bit. So Ian started working with Dad.

The first thing Dad got Ian to help him with was building a shed, because he needed somewhere to keep all his beekeeping equipment. Dad planned out the design he wanted for the shed. They laid out the foundations in an exact square shape. They built it using nine-inch cavity blocks and gave the shed a flat roof with felt covering. The view from on top of the roof of the shed was amazing. Not a road in sight. They put one window on one side of the shed, and another smaller one at the back of the shed. Dad had plans that at some stage he wanted a greenhouse for growing vegetables in, so Ian laid out a platform of cement with more nine-inch cavity blocks around the edge, going up about four blocks. It was a great experience to watch the sand and the cement being shovelled into the cement mixer. Even just to see a cement mixer was a big thing for a young Dub. It was all very exciting.

Sundays. I hated Sundays so much, particularly between Easter and Halloween, when we were only going down to Garryvadden for weekends. Mum would take us to Mass in Blackwater church. It's a lovely church with balconies on either side of the altar and a balcony at the back as well. Dad never went to Mass, partly because he got a bit claustrophobic, and partly I think, because he never really related to what the priest was trying to convey.

We'd come home from Mass and then everything would be go, go, go, getting ready to leave. When we were younger, Mum would have taken care of the packing, but we'd have to help clean the house and hoover. I hate hoovering, although hate is a bit strong. But it's definitely the chore I dislike the most. I actually quite enjoy housework. It's just hoovering. I'm a bit of a perfectionist, and I think getting into all the nooks and crannies is the part that puts me off.

Then Dad would go up to the top corner of the land and go through the bees. This annoyed the bees and made them very cross. It was okay for Dad, because he was covered in his white beekeeping gear. Mum, Peter and myself had to stay inside, or we were sure to be stung. I definitely didn't want to get stung. Not only would it hurt and swell up like it did on everybody else, but I had inherited an allergic reaction to bee stings from my Mum. If one of us got stung, we'd get an awful itch all over our body. All we could do would be to go to bed, take off all our clothes and place a cold sponge on the itchiest parts. This would last about an hour, and we definitely didn't want this to happen when we were planning to head back to Dublin.

When Dad was finished with the bees, we'd load everything into the car and head off. I hated the trip in the car, two hours of car sickness all the way back. When we were back in Dublin I'd go in and lie down on the couch in the sitting room to recover. After that, I might get to run around outside for a bit, then have something to eat and bed pretty soon after that.

One time, Halloween was on a Sunday and we were rushing back to Dublin. I was all worried that we wouldn't have time to get a costume and go around the houses. Mum told me not to worry, but I couldn't stop. When we got home, Mum got to work straight away on a costume for me. In the end, she got out her wedding dress for me to wear. I was thrilled. Mum put some lines of black make-up on my face, and I said to her,

"What am I?"

Mum said, "You're Dracula's bride." I was delighted going around all the houses saying "I'm Dracula's bride."

Other times at Halloween we'd have great fun making popcorn beforehand, and putting it into bags for the children who called at the door. We also used to play the game where we had to take a bite out of the apple in the water, which I was never able to do. We tried the game where we tied the apple to a piece of string as well, but that was even harder.

But this Halloween, things were different. All we had time to do was to go around the houses and get all the apples and nuts and sweets and then go to bed. I don't know if we even got to eat any of the stuff we got from the neighbours.

Chapter 8

Monday morning was an early start, getting ready for school. How I hated Monday mornings. The thought of a whole week of school ahead of me, and another two-hour car journey waiting for me at the end of it was awful. Breakfast was usually Weetabix, and maybe a boiled egg and a slice of toast. I didn't find it the most appetising of breakfasts, but Dad would always say,

"If they're hungry they'll eat it."

I ate it, although there were other cereals I would have preferred, but Weetabix is good for you, so that's what we got. We got a treat of a selection pack on our birthdays, or if we went to stay in a relation's house, or in a hotel or a B&B, then we got a break from the Weetabix. We could have had porridge either. Dad would have a big bowl of porridge every morning with milk and sugar, and he swore by it, said it was the best thing you could eat. I tried it many a time but I never stuck to it. Later on in life I realised it was the milk and sugar that put me off it. I ended up saying that Dad ate lumpy sweet milk. Now I love eating porridge with a spoon of Dad's own honey and a handful of blueberries.

I never really liked the way that Dad cooked the boiled egg for me. I actually quite enjoyed the yolk, although I would have liked it a little less runny, but the thing I hated was the white part, particularly when I got towards the bottom. The white of the egg was nearly liquid in texture. I didn't like it at all but do you think I'd complain? Oh no, I did my best to eat what I was given. That's another reason why I didn't learn very well how to want something for myself. If we're hungry we'll eat it.

After breakfast I had to get my hair done. I quite liked this part of getting ready. Most often I'd ask for two plaits, a ponytail plaited, or maybe a side ponytail plaited. I loved my plaits so much that I'd even ask Mum to do my hair for me at the weekends. I don't remember ever spending much time looking in the mirror and combing or brushing my hair. I never got into the habit of it. I don't think I could ever compete with the way that Mum did my hair, so for years I just let her do it.

Then we'd get our bags and our coats and head outside. Dad would sometimes let Peter have fun revving up the car with the brake on. I remember asking Dad,

Will I be able to drive?"

Dad said "No, because you have epilepsy."

I was quite upset but I kept it to myself. That was another thing I wanted that I couldn't have.

Then, when we were all ready, Mum would drive us up to school. She'd drop us off at about half past eight, and then she'd head on to school herself. I was usually the second person in line. I'd put my bag down and stand in the freezing cold for about half an hour, waiting for the other children and the teachers to come. It was such a relief when the teachers came out to bring us inside. I was so glad to get in out of the cold. I quite liked the roll call. It was a nice routine that I didn't have to worry about, and I wasn't on my own, I was part of the class.

The one part of the school day that I actually liked was lunchtime. It was something I could do by myself and I didn't feel left out, although I have to say that my lunch never satisfied my appetite. I always felt I could have eaten more than I was given, and I didn't really like my sandwich. When I was going to school first, and Mum asked me what I wanted in my sandwich for lunch, I said "Cheese".

Mum said to me "With what?"

I didn't particularly want anything with it but I wasn't confident enough to say what I wanted, so I said,

"ketchup."

I never really liked my cheese and ketchup sandwiches, but I never told anybody. I just ate them because I was hungry.

One of the many things I didn't like about school was when the children had to bring in a present for the teacher at Christmas and at the end of the year. I felt so different, and you know how children like to be the same as everyone else. Mum used to always give me a jar of Dad's honey to give to the teacher. I felt so stupid giving the teacher honey, when all the other children were giving presents nothing like it. Though I have to say my teacher in second class, Mr. Smith, loved Dad's honey. I can remember one child laughing at me giving the honey to the teacher, and Mr. Smith said "Shh".

At one stage in second class, Mum prepared a whole lesson on bees for me to bring in, and she also gave me a little container of honey for all of the children to taste. Mr. Smith did the lesson, but he took the honey home for himself.

I was always teacher's pet when it came to my male teachers. When it came to lining up at the classroom door, ready to go out, Mr. Smith got us into a routine where we were to get into a line of boys and a line of girls. I believe that he did this for me, so that I wouldn't feel so left out at the back of the line by myself. In this way I was part of the group, I was one of the girls.

While Aisling was in the Middle East, two new families moved into our estate, the Hannons and the Suttles. Alex and Julianne Suttle had two boys, Conor and David. By coincidence, David happened to be in Peter's class. They were a lovely family. Now the Hannons were a different story. They had three children . . . Rob, who was a year or two older than me, Ian, who was about a year to a year and a half younger than me, and a younger boy whose name was Chris. Ian became friends with Peter, and Rob became my arch enemy, but Ian wasn't far from being my enemy either, as he called me names. For some reason, Rob had something against me. He would turn up now and then, and just come up and kick me for no reason at all. I was the shy little goody two shoes girl, and would take the kick and just walk away from him.

I remember hanging around with Peter a lot and wishing I could play the games he was playing with his friend. Two of the games in particular that I longed to be able to play were conkers—that would have been in the autumn—and marbles. I used to watch Peter playing top trumps with his friends. I think Peter's pack of top trump cards were tractors, and I played it with him once or twice but I didn't really understand it. Mum made a special marbles bag for Peter with his name sewn onto it. I was so jealous of this I was wishing she'd make something for me.

One thing Mum did make for me was a gorgeous purple dress for me to wear when Peter was making his first Holy Communion. It used to be a dress of hers, and she just made it smaller to fit me. I loved it. I liked the way I looked for Peter's Communion more than I did for my own, as the dress I wore for Peter's fitted me properly. On the Sunday after *I* made my Holy Communion, I remember Mum asking me if I wanted to wear my dress to Mass that day. She said that some girls liked to wear their Communion dress to Mass the following Sunday. I said "No". There was no way I was wearing that dress again. I particularly hated the way the sleeves were too short.

In the summer, one game I really enjoyed was skipping with the big blue rope. Two children would be spinning the rope, and a row of children stood ready and waiting their turn to jump into it one after the other. The skipping game I remember the best was "chase". All I had to be able to do was jump into the rope and jump for a few times and run out. I loved it.

Of course in winter you always had the hope of snow, and the rare few times we had snow I had great fun playing snowballs with the children on the road. I also made one or two snowmen with Peter. The snow was great. I could do without it now though. Oh, the days when I'd look out the window hoping for snow, and hoping that the snow would stick, and the amount of times it didn't was far greater than the times it did. This made the thrill of playing snowballs with all the other children very special. I would feel so much at home playing with the other children on the road, most of whom were boys. I was the same as everyone else and we were like one big family.

Another game I loved was tip the can. It didn't matter if I was shy or had no confidence around people. I loved all the children on my road and really enjoyed playing games like this with them, because I felt like I fitted in. I was well able to hide and try and get to the can without the child who was 'on' seeing me, so that I could free everyone else. These were times in my life when I didn't feel so alone. Although I had a terrifying shadow haunting me, and I never knew when it was going to take me away from everyone, I had all these lovely children nearby, and when the chance came to be one of the crowd, I was in my element.

The time of the day that I hated most in primary school was yard time from 12.30-1.00. I hated this, particularly in the winter when it was freezing cold. I can remember walking around the yard by myself in the cold for half an hour, with my head down kicking stones. One day at yard time, the children were running around on the grass when they shouldn't have been. Mr. Smith was on yard duty so I went up to him. I asked him if I could try and get the children off the grass and he said "Yes". I saw Ian running on the grass so I ran over, grabbed his jumper and pulled him off the grass over to the yard. Ian was quite a small boy so this was no problem for me.

On the way home after school later that day Rob, Ian's older brother, came up to me and kicked me. I just took the kick as usual and kept walking home. Later that day I told Mum about Rob kicking me again. Dad had gone up to Rob many a time before to tell him not to be kicking me, but it hadn't stopped him. Anyway, this time Mum decided to go up to Rob and try telling him again. This time Rob was outside his house and Mum walked towards him and I followed her. Just as Mum was about to talk to Rob, his father, Daniel came out of their house. Daniel was a teacher and he walked up to us to find out what was going on. Mum told Daniel that Rob had kicked me. When Daniel heard this he was furious, and he started smacking Rob on the back of the neck. I can still remember Rob running into his house with his father chasing after him, smacking him continuously on the back of the neck. At the time I was in my element. It was the best day of my life. Rob never once kicked or bothered me again after that. I remember Mum feeling really guilty though, which didn't please me at all. I so felt he deserved it.

Before Aisling went away, I tried out ballet with her after school. That didn't last very long, and I don't know if I even went to two classes. Of course I would never have had the posture for ballet at that time in my life. My head was down so much because I was shy, or because I was miserable and didn't feel loved or wanted. I had no confidence at all.

At Easter, Aisling used to get about nine Easter eggs from all her aunts, whereas I'd only get one, which would be gone on Easter Sunday. A few days after Easter, Aisling would be complaining about all the chocolate she had and the number of Easter eggs. This really got on my nerves. Inside I would have been thinking to myself, '*give them to me and I'll eat them for you*', but I never said anything and she never offered them to me either.

Chapter 9

Back down to Garryvadden on Friday evening. How I hated the trip down. I would have much preferred to be watching Bosco and Fortycoats, which is what I must have done during the winter months.

While we were down in Wexford, Dad would sometimes be sawing, and he'd get me to hold the wood while he sawed. I found this quite interesting at first, but after a while I'd get tired of it.

Up at the boundary of our land there were rabbit burrows which fascinated me. Every time we saw one of the many little rabbits scurrying about, it gave us a great thrill. They were so beautiful and so perfect.

The Easter bunny started coming to us some time after Mum and Dad bought Garryvadden. On Holy Saturday, Peter and myself would write letters to the Easter bunny telling him what Easter egg we wanted. We'd give our letters to Dad and he'd go up to the boundary and put our letters in the top burrow, where I was certain the Easter bunny lived. On Easter Sunday morning, Mum would take Peter and myself to Mass in Blackwater, and when we came home Dad would be up and the four of us would have a big fry-up for breakfast. Of course Peter and myself were all excited waiting for the Easter bunny to come with our Easter eggs. We'd keep running into the sitting room to check the fireplace, as that's where the Easter bunny always left our two eggs, sitting perfectly on top of the mantelpiece, one on either side. Sometime after breakfast, we'd find that he'd left us our eggs. They'd be gone in no time though, down the red lane. I used to savour mine for as long as I could but I'd say it definitely didn't last more than an hour.

One Easter, Dad was running a course in Wexford as part of his work, so it was just Mum, Peter and myself in Garryvadden by ourselves. One of the days, the cows across the lane were making an awful racket altogether, mooing non-stop. At one stage Mum said to Peter and myself,

"Go over and see what's up with the cows."

So Peter and myself headed out the gate and across the lane to the big metal gate. We climbed up a few bars on the gate and looked down to where the cows were. We saw that it was actually a small group of lovely young calves that were making all the noise. Then Peter said to me,

"Look, one of the calves is lying on the ground."

I couldn't see properly, so we climbed over the gate and made our way over to have a better look. When we got there, we saw that one of the calves had got himself all caught up in a metal feeder, and his head was stuck between the bars.

We ran back up to the gate, climbed back over it, and made our way back to Mum. We didn't know what was going to happen because we had no car, so we couldn't go to tell Bill O'Brien, who had bought the land off Alex Kelly. After we told Mum, she said "We'll walk over to Ned".

So off we went up the hill looking for Ned Kelly. He must have been up at the house because I don't recall having any problem finding him. Anyway, we informed Ned of the situation and the four of us all headed back down the lane and in to where the calf was trapped on the ground, all tangled up in the feeder.

I found it so entertaining to watch Ned pull and tug at the poor calf for at least five minutes trying to get it out, especially the way he grabbed the calf's ears. It really seemed quite amazing to me and it was lovely to see the poor calf trot off to join the other calves, when Ned finally managed to get it out of the feeder. Then Ned went off to let Bill know what had happened.

That Easter Sunday afternoon, we had an unexpected visit from Bill O'Brien and his wife. They had come to thank us for saving their calf and they brought two Cadbury's Flake Easter eggs with them, one for Peter and one for myself. We were thrilled. We kept thanking Bill and his wife loads of times, because it was a lovely surprise, and so unusual for us to get *two* Easter eggs. That had never happened before. Saving the calf was a fabulous adventure for me, and even that on its own would have made Easter special for me, but to get another Easter egg, wow. What a special Easter that was.

Bill had done great work to the land across the road. He was a much better farmer than Alex, who had Parkinson's disease, which really restricted what he could do. Though we nearly preferred the way the land was when Alex owned it. It was actually very bad land, all marshy, particularly as you went down nearer the river where all the trees were. Dad used to take Peter and myself over to 'the forest', as we called it, as a little adventure.

There used to be an electric fence that we had to go under to get into the main part of the field. This seemed quite scary to me, but Dad would just say,

"You'll be fine, don't worry".

Walking in my wellington boots through the trees in the marsh was really quite exciting, but my favourite was when I got stuck in the marsh and I had to get Dad to pull me out. It was like being in the middle of a tug of war between Dad and the squelchy land, and Dad always won even if I lost a boot and he had to pull that out after me.

After Bill bought the land from Alex, he drained it, and cut down all of the trees near the river. He also got a new pump for the well, which hardly gave us any trouble after that. He painted the big barn a blue/grey colour and he got a slurry pit put into it. He had it done very professionally so it was covered up, and no little children could fall into it and die.

One of Lily's grandsons Kevin, when he was very small, fell into the slurry pit on the farm where he was from. He could have died only for the fact that Sandra, Lily's daughter, stuck her arm into the slurry exactly where Kevin had fallen in, and pulled him out. He was, and still, is just fine thank God.

When we were down in Garryvadden over the summer, my aunts, uncles and cousins would come and stay with us for a few days. Peter and myself would have great fun with our cousins altogether. It was always a great thrill to hear that we were having visitors, even if it did mean we had to help tidy the house and do work outside as well.

There was a little bridge about half a mile down the hill and Dad, Peter and myself, would walk down to the bridge with our cousins, and walk into the water in our wellington boots and explore in underneath the bridge. The bridge had about five little arches that we could go into, two of which had very little water flowing into them. We'd see eels swimming in the water, which was a bit scary at first but once Dad reassured us that they wouldn't harm us, we were fine. There were also little minnows swimming around. Peter and myself would make homemade nets out of metal clothes hangers and old tights. We'd catch the little minnows and bring them home in jam jars. They'd just end up dying of course, just like the tadpoles, but it was a great thrill to catch them anyway.

Back up in Dublin I was having a hard time with Ian. He kept calling me "Bummy", which rhymed with our surname. The thing that got to me the most was that even though Peter had the same name as me, he didn't get called "Bummy". I used to hang around with Peter because I had no other friends, and I think this was Ian's way of trying to get rid of me. I'll tell you something though, it really hurt me not being able to hang around with my own brother without getting bullied by his best friend, and Peter would never have said anything to Ian, he'd just let him bully me away.

The dining room in our house was like our playroom, with a relatively small amount of toys in it. Rusty the rocking-horse was my favourite toy that I ever had and I was so disappointed when I had to give it away to my younger cousin Sarah. Sometimes, when we were having my grandparents over for dinner, for example, we'd have to help tidy the house. I wouldn't call Mum the most dedicated of housekeepers. Anyway we'd have to collect up all the toys, put them into a cardboard box and move them into another room. Then the big table would be pulled out and opened up and we'd have to help set it for dinner, which I actually quite enjoyed.

My grandparents loved playing the card game bridge, and they'd play it with my parents. I used to watch them play from a very young age, and over the years I picked it up and became a very good player myself.

After Betty had been minding us for a few years, she became pregnant and had to leave us. What happened then was that Peter and myself would be left in the house by ourselves for the hour after school until Mum got home. We were told not to go outside, or to open the front door to anybody. My main memory of this time was standing at the window with Peter, looking out and waiting for Mum to come home.

One Christmas when I was writing my letter to Santa Claus, I asked him for a puppy. I was sitting at the kitchen table, and Mum was standing over at the sink. When she heard that I was asking Santa for a puppy she said to me,

"What if Santa doesn't bring you a puppy?"

I said, "He will, Santa will give me anything I want".

In a way it's funny that I said that, because usually when I woke up on Christmas day, I hadn't got what I'd asked for, but I never complained. I was just glad to get anything and was always very grateful.

One particular evening when I went into the dining room, I found Peter inside with Ian. Ian was trying to persuade Peter that Santa was actually our Mum and Dad, but Peter wasn't convinced. Then I joined into the argument, because I was so convinced that Santa was real.

Peter and myself were arguing with Ian saying things like,

"How would our parents be able to afford this?" We were pointing at a miniature trampoline.

"Sure Mum won't even let me have a Barbie doll."

"When we go shopping, buying presents for other children always seems to be more important than buying presents/toys for me."

In the end, I was so confident that Santa wasn't Mum and Dad that I said to Ian,

"Ok then, I'll ask Mum". So off I went into the kitchen to confirm that my parents weren't Santa.

"Are you and Dad Santa?" I asked Mum.

Her answer was, "I think you should talk to your Dad about that, he's in the sitting room".

When I went into the sitting room, Dad was down on his knees lighting the fire. I said straight out to him,

"Dad, are you Santa?"

Dad replied to me, "Well Sarah, I think it's time you knew".

I was ten years of age at the time. I was stunned. It felt like my world had caved in. I turned around to leave the room but then I poked my head back in and said to Dad,

"I suppose you're the Easter bunny and the tooth fairy too", and walked off quite upset but no tears.

Ian didn't manage to persuade Peter, but he'd made my imaginary world cave in. I felt so alone.

When we first got the house in Garryvadden, the land was all uneven, so Dad got it levelled and planted fresh grass. I remember helping Dad to plant Leylandii trees at the far boundary. Dad said to me,

"These trees will grow nice and tall and they'll make the bees fly higher so that they won't get caught in your hair".

I asked Dad how long it would take them to grow. He said,

"About ten to fifteen years".

My excitement disappeared and I thought to myself, that's too long sure my life will be over by then. Dad grew lovely Golden Leylandii at the front border out onto the lane.

Peter and myself had great fun climbing trees down in Garryvadden. There was one tree in particular at the back of the shed that Peter and myself would spend quite some time in. One day we were up in this tree and we noticed a swarm of bees just behind me. We climbed down out of the tree and went to tell Dad. He came along with a box and just tipped the swarm into the box. Dad was delighted with this as he could make another beehive out of this. There was lots of clover on our land and in loads of the fields around us. The bees worked the clover and made lots of clover honey for us. I hated the time of year when Dad took the honey off the bees and Mum had to extract it from the frames. I don't know how she did it to be honest with you, it looked so sticky and messy and she did it in the kitchen so the kitchen ended up being all sticky.

Dad made a tyre swing for us off one of the trees near the entrance to the property. I loved swinging on it. It was great!! One day I was walking around the land, dodging the thistles which were growing in quite a lot of areas up in the top half of the land. Anyway, I was walking along and I noticed a nest with little eggs in it. Dad told me that it was probably a pheasant's nest. We'd often see pheasants even as we were driving along the lane. It was mostly female pheasants, which were the brown ones, but the odd time we might see a cock pheasant which was nice, they were lovely and colourful to attract the females and it didn't matter so much if they got shot as they play no part in rearing their young.

Mum and Dad both loved gardening, and one of the phases Mum went through was growing strawberries. I used to have fun helping her grow her strawberries. We had to cut the runners, which were kind of like little tubes coming out of the main plant to grow little babies. Anyway, we'd have to cut the runners and maybe plant them again into the bottom half of milk cartons. That's what Mum had decided to use instead of pots, probably because there were so many of them and she couldn't afford to buy lots of pots. Then there came the time of the year when we had to pick the strawberries. As a reward, what we got from all this quite enjoyable work was lovely homemade strawberry jam . . . Delicious. Dad also planted raspberries and we had to help pick them too, but I don't remember anything Mum made with the raspberries. We probably just ate them with ice cream. There was another time of the year when all the blackberries came out all along the lane. We'd go picking them as well and Mum would make apple and blackberry crumble with them.

At some stage during our time down in Garryvadden, Dad, Peter and myself discovered mushrooms growing in one of Ian Kelly's fields. We used to have great fun walking around Ian's field picking a huge selection of lovely big mushrooms. When we started picking them I said to Dad.

"Will they poison us?"

Dad said, "These ones are fine".

He told me that he'd picked mushrooms as a child. I was quite satisfied with this and went around the field thoroughly enjoying collecting lots of lovely mushrooms.

When we got back, Dad used to stuff the mushrooms with breadcrumbs, garlic, onion and maybe some herbs as well, and then cook them under the grill. They were delicious. After a while, Ian discovered that we were picking all his mushrooms, so he ploughed up the field to stop them growing and that was the end of our mushroom picking.

At one stage, Dad started divining for water. He felt we shouldn't be relying on the water from across the road, and that it would be better if we had our own water. One day, he got a man in a digger to dig down in a certain area on our land where he'd got some indication that there might be water. The digger went down as far as he could go, but no luck. Then Dad did more divining, and found that there seemed to be water in the area under the tyre swing, so he decided to dig a well himself.

I was devastated to hear that we'd have to get rid of the tyre swing because I loved it. Dad said we'd make another tyre swing somewhere else but we never did. Anyway, Dad started digging the well and he got Sean, the man up the hill in the little cottage, to make cement rings to line the well as he went down. Sean had dug a well himself previously so he knew about the rings. As Dad went down, Peter and myself had great fun playing with the sand that he'd be digging up. Dad would have been down deep in the ground and Mum, Peter and myself would be up at ground level. It was actually quite a nice activity that the family enjoyed doing together.

Dad made a tripod, first out of wood and then a better one out of metal. He made a pulley to pass the soil, sand and marl up to Mum in the bucket, so Mum could empty it out for us to play with. Dad ended up with a well with about three feet of water, and he was very proud of his well that he'd dug himself. Later on, Dad made a lovely flowerbed all around the well and down the hill towards the gate. He had chosen a lovely selection of different plants and placed bark mulch over the soil to keep down the weeds. It looked beautiful.

I was still having seizures on and off throughout my life. I was going to Dr. McMenamin in Our Lady's Children's Hospital in Crumlin at this stage. Dad would take me out of school at certain times in the year and bring me to this man. I didn't know what was happening at the time. Of course I loved being taken out of school, any reason to get out of school and I'd be thrilled. I loved this little adventure, particularly when the doctor made me walk in a straight line, one foot in front of the other, or when he got me to touch my nose and then touch his finger when he placed it in different positions in front of my eyes.

I was old enough to take medication now. The tablets, which I was taking three times a day, were called Epilim. The only problem was remembering to take them, particularly in the middle of the day. There were quite a number of times when I forgot to take them, and if I didn't take them I'd probably have a seizure. They weren't stopping the seizures completely, but they were keeping them at bay, to a certain extent. I loved these visits to the doctor, but I never knew that my dad was forking out fifty pounds every time.

Having epilepsy was horrible. I felt so different and so left out. It was holding me back so much in school as well. I don't know how often I would have had seizures in the first ten years of my life . . . maybe every two months. I'd collapse on the ground and start shaking for a minute and a half, and then go asleep for half an hour.

Of course nobody knew what I was going through, as they watched my body shake and shake. I was going through hell for a minute and a half, all by myself. It was awful. I'd get this horrible feeling coming over me, which would last about thirty seconds. Then I was gone. I was in the dark all by myself, with this terrifying feeling of having nobody there for me, knowing nobody could help me. This was my life and I had no control over it.

There was nothing I could do about it. I just had to learn to live with it but that definitely wasn't easy to do. It was stopping me making friends. It was stopping me opening up to people. It was keeping me closed in on myself and getting me down. It was messing up my brain, because each time I had a seizure my memory got pretty badly messed up, and it would take a few days to pull itself back together again.

It's gas though, even though I hated school, I actually loved my *own* school. I was proud to be a pupil in St. Colmcille's Primary School. I'm not sure why, I guess because it was a big part of who I was. Even though I hardly talked to anyone, I was still one of the group.

I loved the times of the year when we, the pupils, had to raise money for the school. Someone had come up with the idea of a sponsored 'skip', where every pupil was given an A4 sheet of card with lines and sections made out for the names of the people who were going to sponsor them. Mum always started the sheet off by sponsoring me for one pound, no matter how many skips I did, and everyone else I asked to sponsor me did the same. I loved going around the houses and asking the neighbours to sponsor me. They were all so nice and I don't remember anyone who said "No" or closed the door on me.

There was also the sponsored 'spell', where the pupils had to get as many spellings correct as they could, instead of skipping for as long as they could. It was such a big school that it was divided into two buildings, one for junior infants to second class, and the other building for third class to sixth class. There were prefabs as well, and since there were so many pupils, we'd raise loads of money.

Another time that I felt really at home in school was if for some reason they played the national anthem over the intercom. I would stand up with everyone else and I'd be so proud to be Irish. But I hated learning Irish, because I was pathetic at it. I hated history as well, as it was something I couldn't picture at all. I don't think I had much of an imagination. You see I don't think I had enough confidence to be imaginative of my own accord. The subjects I loved were art and PE. One of the reasons I loved the day we had PE was because we got to wear our tracksuit into school on that day, so I wasn't freezing out in the cold without my legs covered.

I loved running around with the other pupils. This was another opportunity for me to be one of the group, although I never ended up being very good at anything really, because of my social skills. I remember calling for someone to pass the basketball to me, but no one would ever pass it to me. I loved sports so much though. I tried playing camogie with the school but I didn't last very long. I don't think I got much further than just hitting the sliotar along the ground with the stick to one of the other players. I'd seen hurling being played on television and I don't think I had the patience for it. I think I found it a bit boring as well, not enough running around. My social skills would have held me back here as well.

In third class, my teacher's name was Miss Cassin, and she was really nice to me. Not only did she not give us homework on Fridays, but she didn't give us any homework on Tuesdays either.

In the senior school, they had a special teacher to help with the children's reading. Miss Cassin sent myself and another lovely girl whose name was Amy Plunkett to this lady Mrs McCorry once a week. This really helped my reading, but I'd say my reading went downhill again the following year when I didn't have any help or motivation for it. I became friends with Amy, but I was still really shy and I don't think we spent much time together outside of school.

While Aisling was away in the Middle East, I used to spend time with a girl called Orla. Her family had moved into one of the houses further up the road in our estate, and she was in Peter's class. I used to go up to Orla and I'd be invited into the house. Then Orla, her mother, her two younger brothers and myself would go into the TV room and watch the DJ cat show on the television for what seemed like hours. I didn't like the DJ cat show at all, because I found it quite boring. But I was glad of the company and was very polite, so I didn't say anything, I just sat with them. I have hardly any memory of playing outside with Orla.

One of the very few days I *was* outside with Orla, Aisling turned up out of the blue. She was home!! I was so excited that I instinctively left Orla, without saying a word to her, and headed straight for Aisling. I don't know what I said to Aisling or what we did afterwards. It's a bit of a blur really. I'll tell you something though, I'll never forget what resulted from me leaving Orla to go to Aisling. It was one big, bad mistake.

I can still remember very clearly what happened later that night. I was sitting in the armchair with my head down on the arm, and my face looking straight into it, in tears. My parents were giving out to me and insisting that I apologise to Orla. Orla hadn't said anything to me since I'd left her earlier that day . . . not to say that we ever talked that much. I don't know if either of Orla's parents had said anything to my parents. Maybe they had, and maybe that's why my parents were so mad at me. I was in bits. Mum and Dad were adamant that I should apologise to Orla, but I couldn't see what I'd done wrong. I mean if Orla had come up to me and said something to me then fine, I'd apologise to her, but in my eyes Orla didn't seem to be hurt at all.

I really didn't want to apologise to her, not because I was afraid of apologising, I just couldn't see the point of it. If I was to apologise it should be for the benefit of Orla and myself, not my parents. Looking back at it now, Orla's parents must have said something to mine. I never experienced anything like this with my parents before or after this incident. In the end, I agreed that I'd apologise to Orla. I really didn't have much choice in the matter.

I remember standing with Orla at the wall outside our house and saying to her "I'm sorry". I don't know if I said what I was sorry for, or why I did whatever I'd done wrong, but I can definitely remember saying 'Sorry' again and again. Orla just kept saying to me,

"My daddy told me never to talk to you again".

I began to feel like I should be apologising to her dad instead, because Orla didn't seem to be annoyed with me at all. Before this incident, anytime I saw Orla's dad driving in his car he'd always wave at me and I'd always wave back, but after this he barely looked at me. I definitely think it was Orla's dad who had the problem with me and not Orla. In the end, I think Orla said "Ok" to me, but we never really spent much time with each other after that.

Chapter 12

One of the hobbies I tried while I was in the senior school was playing the tin whistle. Mum bought one for me and I went to a few classes. I remember practising 'Twinkle, twinkle little star' on my own. Mum and Dad never really listened to me or encouraged me to play it for them, but I must have enjoyed playing it, because I played 'Twinkle twinkle' so well that I got twenty pence as a reward from the teacher. I never really saw the point of it after that and I didn't go to any more classes. Mum and Dad never really asked me why I didn't want to go anymore. Maybe if they had, I would have kept it up, who knows.

I still hated school. I hated school so much that as I was sitting in the classroom in my own little world, I'd be hoping and hoping that someday the school would go on fire so I wouldn't have to go to school anymore. It never occurred to me that I'd have to go to a different school though. Every time the fire alarm went off it was just another fire drill, which meant we had to go out into the cold, which I hated. I'd actually be hoping for rain as well. That would mean that we wouldn't have to go outside for yard time, we'd be kept inside instead.

When it came to the subjects, I was so bad at everything except art. I was one of the best in the class when it came to art, but pretty much everything else I was really bad at. My brother Peter, on the other hand, would have been one of the top of the class at his work. He was so much better at socialising as well. He would have had loads of friends at school, but unfortunately he didn't really get to socialise much with them outside of school because of Wexford, and Mum not being at home when we got home from school. He probably went to his friend's birthday parties too, though I'm not sure about that. I hardly went to anybody's birthday party, or at least if I did I wouldn't have enjoyed it much. I'd always have been left out and by myself. There was just one time when I invited girls from my class to my birthday party, but I hardly spoke to one of them. I think they had a better time than I did. Other times it would have just been the children from around the estate.

There was a sports day in school every summer, probably in June, which I loved. Of all of them, there's only one sports day that I remember very clearly. It was because of a certain incident that happened.

I was standing around on the green on my own, where everyone was getting ready for the egg and spoon race. Then, out of nowhere, this boy came up to me. He was holding a big, stainless steel spoon in his hand. Now when I say big I mean big. It was huge. The boy said to me,

"Do you own this?"

Now, I'm not one to lie, but when I saw this spoon I just stared at it and said,

"Yes".

I walked the egg and spoon race after that and got a lovely gold medal as a prize, but to this very day, I still feel guilty because it wasn't my spoon and I know that I wouldn't have won with a normal dessert spoon.

There was something very special for me about the month of June. Mum would be there when I got home from school, because she taught in a secondary school and was on holidays in June, July and August. It was always lovely to come home to Mum. I had someone to share my misery with, to some extent anyway. I remember one time I was complaining to Mum about my life and having to do homework, and that I didn't understand the reason for it.

I was saying things like,

"Why do we get homework? Why do I have to have epilepsy? It's not fair!!

Mum replied,

"Sarah, life isn't fair. You have a lot of things going for you".

I said "What? What could be worse than having epilepsy?"

Mum's answer was "You're not blind".

I was speechless. I thought to myself, she's right. Maybe I have no real friends, maybe nobody knows what I'm going through all on my own, but at least I can see.

This made me think about all the things that a person who was blind from birth would never be able to experience . . . What I had that they didn't have . . . All the things we take so much for granted . . . The things that bring me closest to God our father, the things that no scientist or doctor can give a reason for.

Why does the first daffodil in the front garden bring so much joy to my heart in springtime? Why does a rainbow lift up my spirits and fill my heart with happiness on a wet and miserable day? Oh yes, they can tell us how a rainbow appears, but can they explain the joy it brings to all the people who see it? The list is endless in my opinion. It just goes on and on. Maybe you could thank God for a tree, but don't forget the buds on the tree in spring. I love the buds of the tree and the buds lead to the leaves, and the leaves lead to colour and design these things we take so much for granted, and I think it's quite sad that we don't appreciate them more.

My friend says to me,

"You like Mass? Why do you like Mass?"

I like Mass because I have a huge faith in God. I have been able to feel God inside me since I was twenty-six years of age. I can feel God inside me when I'm saying the creed of faith. I love it. I feel how proud God is of me when I recite it with such confidence. I would never see or feel anything special in the host . . . that's just routine to me and it's just wafer, there's no feeling from it. I suppose if I was to look for feeling in it, it would be the pleasure of eating it, but it's hard to get pleasure from a tiny piece of wafer.

Though within that routine, I have my own routine. When I'm on my knees before I receive communion, I pray to my dad, my uncles, my aunt and my step-grandmother Lily. I pray to these people to connect with their closest, living loved ones, all of whom are members of either my family, or of my extended family. That's another part of the Mass that I love because I feel so close to my dad and my deceased family members. When I'm kneeling down after I have received the body of Christ, I start to thank the Lord. I list off as many things as I can think of to thank him for, including food and drink, and when I run out of things I say to God

"Thank you most of all for the things I have forgotten to thank you for".

Like my eyes . . . I never remember to thank him for my eyes. So then when it comes to the end of the Mass, and we all say "Thanks be to God", I know why I came to Mass.

When I try to share my faith with people verbally, I can feel fear inside me and my heart starts pounding. I get very nervous because I know nobody is going to understand. Writing it down is so much easier. The written word we can see and feel, so I can portray my feelings for you to see and not be nervous about what you think of my experience of God.

We'd still be heading down to Wexford on a very regular basis. Dad would keep most of his holidays for the summer, and as soon as Peter and myself were finished school, we'd head down to Wexford and stay there for five weeks. I remember saying to Mum and Dad,

"I wish we could stay in Dublin for the summer".

Dad would reply,

"Sure there's nobody here in the summer anyway".

I'd just take their word for it and wouldn't go on about it anymore.

I hated leaving Dublin so much. I think the journey made it ten times worse though. Once we got down to Garryvadden it wasn't so bad, particularly in the summer when we wouldn't have another journey two days later heading back up to Dublin. When we were just going down for the weekends, it felt like I spent more time in the car than out of it. Suffering nearly four hours of car sickness within three days seemed like an eternity for me. When I was in the car I used to feel like the journey was never going to end.

At some stage while we were down in Garryvadden, we found out that we could buy eggs from the Kellys—Ned Kelly, his sister and his mother, who lived just up the hill. Their hens produced the most gorgeous, big eggs with lovely orange yolks, and they only charged us fifty pence for half a dozen.

They showed us a quicker way to get down to their house. Instead of walking all the way up Garryvadden lane, and then going down the long, dark narrow lane with big tall trees on either side, they showed us a way through their fields instead. We'd just walk up Garryvadden lane a little bit, until we came to a relatively small wooden gate with a metal hook at the side. We'd unhook the gate and lift it over a bit so we could get through. Peter and myself would walk into a big field of grass that sometimes had cows in it.

Nearly as soon as we walked in the gate we were on a slope. It was lovely walking down the hill surrounded by lots of lovely green grass. When we got down to the bottom of the hill, the land levelled out and we'd walk up to another wooden gate on the left-hand side. This bigger gate lead into another fairly big field that sloped uphill on the left-hand side, but was pretty level straight in front of us. Then we'd walk straight across the field to a little white gate that opened onto a small yard in front of a reasonable sized house.

Mum would always give me a bag with egg cartons to bring with us when we went to buy eggs from Mrs. Kelly. Peter and myself found Mrs. Kelly's house absolutely fascinating. It was a very old style country house and really quite unique. When we walked in the front door, there was a wall with a little window straight in front of us. It was a very unusual type of window as it was just like a pane of glass fourteen inches down by about eight inches across. Behind the glass the wall started to retreat, as the gap between the walls got thinner. The little rectangular tunnel went in about six inches away from us. It was kind of like a giant spy hole. You could see out through it from the inside but you couldn't really see in from the doorway.

There was one door on the left and one door on the right. We were never brought into the room on the left. I think it might have been like a sitting room. We were always brought in through the door on the right into what I'd suppose you'd call the living room. This room had a narrow staircase along the wall to the left. Around the corner to the left there was a big fireplace. Mrs. Kelly would be sitting in the far corner under the stairs beside the bellows, and every so often she'd turn the bellows to keep the fire going. The place where she sat was straight across from the little window so she had a perfect view if anyone came to visit. Over the other side of the room there was a dresser up against the wall on the right.

Mrs. Kelly had three children, Joan who took care of the house and Ned who worked the farm of mainly cattle. I remember walking across the fields at different times of the year. At one time of year there'd be bullocks in the first field eating the grass. At another time the field was just full of grass that had grown so high it was up to our knees. It was quite hard walking through this long grass. Then there was the time of the year when there were bales of hay in the field.

When we started going over through the fields first, the bales of hay were a rectangular shape, and they'd be tilted up against other bales to let them dry out. As the years went on, the rectangular bales turned into Swiss roll bales. One summer, my cousin Richard came down to stay with us for a week. Richard, Peter and myself would go over to the Kelly's to play around their farm. One day, we were up in the first field and there were loads of Swiss roll bales all over the place. The three of us started pushing the bales around the field. Then all of a sudden, one of the bales started rolling faster and faster down the hill and ended up in the ditch at the bottom of the field. I'd say we spent about five minutes trying to pull the bale out of the ditch, with no success.

Mrs. Kelly had one other child, her daughter Ellen. Ellen had been the only one of Mrs. Kelly's three children to get married. She married a man called Bill Lynch, and they made up for her other two children by having thirteen children, ten girls and three boys including one set of twins, a boy and a girl. One summer Mrs. Kelly invited Peter and myself over to the house to meet her grandchildren. We met Ian, who was about three years older than me, Lizzy who was about a year older than me, and May who was a few months younger than me. The five of us got on very well right from the start.

Behind the house there was a big area which was a mixture of stones and soil, and that's where all the hens were wandering around. There might have been a gate leading into this area in the past, as there was a pillar at the far left side as you walked around the house. There were three outhouses on the left-hand side, down from the pillar—two small out-houses and one pretty sizable one.

One of the games the five of us played was tip the can. We made the pillar the can, and I remember having great fun altogether as there were so many places where we could hide. Sometimes we might find an egg or two lying around and it was a lovely experience bringing it into Joan and saying "I found an egg". Another thing I remember doing with Lizzy was plaiting the string that was in the big out-house—the string that would be used to make the bales of hay. I remember the first plait I did. I did it with blue, yellow and orange string. I thought it looked lovely. The second one I did with two blue and one yellow. This plait didn't have the same effect as the first, being made of only two colours instead of three.

At about three o'clock, Joan would call the five of us to come in for the tea. She'd bring us in through the living room into a little room at the back of the house. This room consisted mainly of a fairly sizable table in the shape of a rectangle. There were two benches on either side of the table with no backs on them. We'd all be poured a cup of tea from the pot and there'd be lovely fresh milk, probably straight from the cow that morning, and sugar if you wanted it. There'd be slices of Joan's lovely homemade brown bread for us, buttered with butter she probably made herself, and covered in raspberry jam. It was lovely.

One time Ned brought one of his cows into one of the smaller outhouses to be milked. I watched Lizzy take a turn at doing it, and she was brilliant, so she'd obviously done it before. Then there was the other cow that was brought in to feed her calves. Peter and myself found it very entertaining watching the two calves lowering the milk as it bubbled up around their mouths.

Lizzy, May and Ian used to come over to play around our land as well. We would have had our bikes down for the summer and Lizzy and May weren't able to cycle. Lizzy was trying to cycle my bike and

May kept asking Lizzy to give her a go. I thought to myself, if either of them were going to learn how to cycle on my bike, they'd need quite some time with the bike on their own, so I kept out of it and let Lizzy teach herself to cycle, which she did. Ian was cycling away on Peter's bike, showing off by holding out one arm while he was cycling. I thought to myself, that's easy, I can do that. At some stage I got stung by a honeybee and had to go inside. Mum brought me into her room and I lay on the bed while she sponged me. I had to stay inside for an hour, itching unbearably, and wishing the whole time that I could be playing outside with the others.

Chapter 14

By this time, we had a lovely big lawn in front, and to the right-hand side of the house in Garryvadden. Dad, Peter and myself used to get great enjoyment from kicking a football around with each other on this lovely lawn. On the downside, Peter and myself were given the delightful job of mowing the lawn between us for our pocket money, which was a real pain. We mustn't have been given that much pocket money anyway, as I can't remember getting very excited about it.

The one thing I do remember about my pocket money is to do with weekends in Dublin. When I was younger, Peter and myself would walk with Dad to the newsagents just up the road from where we lived, on a Saturday morning. I was allowed twenty-five pence on Saturday and twenty-five pence on Sunday. I remember Dad getting a bit impatient as he waited for us to decide what we wanted. We'd be trying to get the best value of sweets for our twenty-five pence. Maybe I should have said to Dad that if he gave us an extra five pence I'd be able to buy a lovely bar of chocolate, and he wouldn't have had to wait long at all, but I never said anything. I just tried to make the best of what I was given.

Down in Garryvadden, Dad used to spend a lot of time up in what we called the veg patch, which was basically a lot of soil, further over to the right of the lawn. Dad had dug up this soil and turned it a lot, so there weren't too many weeds in it. But further up to the right from it, there was more soil with loads of weeds, particularly thistles and nettles. I used to work with Dad in the veg patch, picking up weeds as he dug the soil. I remember Dad digging the trenches for the potatoes, and after he'd dug them he'd put manure into them that he would have got from Bill. Bill had a big pile of manure across the road and had told Dad to take as much as he wanted. I was given the job of putting down the seed potatoes on top of the manure in the trenches. After I'd put down the potatoes in one trench, Dad would cover them over with soil that he'd dug up as he made the next trench. Then we'd start the process all over again.

Planting the potatoes would have taken the most time and effort, but of all the vegetables that we planted, the potatoes always turned out the best. No, actually the onions turned out the best. Dad used to grow the most gorgeous sweet onions, and I loved them. He also planted lettuce, which grew very well for him. The carrots were lovely too, the only problem being that they never grew that big. One time when I was up in the veg patch with Dad, I saw a rabbit with myxomatosis. It was so sad. He was quite a big rabbit, his head was swollen and his eyes were very bulbous, but he was just sitting there hardly moving at all. He didn't react to any movement Dad or myself made. He only took one hop when I went up close to him.

On Saturday mornings in Garryvadden, Dad would drive into Blackwater to buy The Irish Times. The shops in Blackwater were pretty bad, and quite often by the time we got to Blackwater, all of the papers would be gone. If there were no papers in Blackwater, Dad would drive to Kilmuckridge, which was just a few miles away and had a much better shop. Quite often, after Dad had got the paper he'd drive us to Blackwater beach, on the Kilmuckridge side of Blackwater. This wasn't my favourite beach, and I don't know if we ever went swimming there, but it was perfect for a walk on a Saturday morning.

Sometimes Dad would just drive there, and sit in the car looking out at the waves. There was a big area where you could park your car, with loads of stones in front of you leading down to the beach. There was a cliff on the left-hand side and a river on the right. In the summer they used to put up a bridge so you could get across to the other side where there was also a cliff. There were no dunes on this beach, but Dad, Peter and myself would have great fun skimming stones on the sea. It was very hard because of all the waves, and a lot of the time I wouldn't be able to do it. Sometimes though, I managed to do two or three skims, and it was a great thrill when I did.

During the summer when we had our bikes with us, the three of us would go cycling together. Mum never came with us as she couldn't cycle very well. Sometimes we'd go for a cycle around the block, which was about three miles and quite hilly. Other times we'd cycle into Blackwater, which was about the same distance and also hilly.

One time, my Uncle James, God rest his soul, and my Aunt Sylvia and their three youngest children Jason, Ciaran and Brian dropped into us on their way back from France. We rarely saw them as they lived in Castlebar in Co. Mayo, so it was a great surprise. Jason fell asleep in one of the chairs in the sitting room not long after they arrived. It was pretty late and they were very tired after their journey, so we didn't do much that night.

The next day we headed into Blackwater, and went to the arcade there. Dad had taken Peter and myself to this arcade many times previously to entertain us. When we first went there, it was located behind Etchingham's pub, the main pub in Blackwater. To the right side of the pub there was a little pathway along by the river. We'd go down the path a bit, and then in on the left there was a smallish room with a good few arcade games, which took ten pence pieces at the time. Peter really took to one game in particular called "Ghosts and goblins" and he became very good at it.

After a number of years the man who ran the arcade, mainly for the summer months, moved his location up the hill a bit. It was like a big barn with a little café to the right-hand side, much bigger than the original arcade. It was a much better location as well, because anyone who was driving through Blackwater village from the Kilmuckridge direction would see it. As a result, he expanded his business big time. There were quite a few machines that you put coins in to try and win more coins in return, and I remember the twenty pence piece coming into use.

There were two or three pool tables there. I remember playing a lot of pool with Peter and I became very good at it. Peter was a great teacher and a great role model. But the main attraction for Peter was the two full size snooker tables. In those days, Peter had a great passion for snooker. He got his first snooker table when he was three years of age, a small one that you could fit on any reasonable sized table. Then when he was about seven or eight, he asked Santa for a snooker table. Mum and Dad got him a second-hand pool table with a set of snooker balls. At this stage, I didn't believe in Santa any more, but I can still remember lying in bed that Christmas Eve and listening to Mum and Dad trying to carry the pool table up the stairs. I was holding back the laughter as I heard Mum cursing and swearing trying to lift it.

Peter was a really good snooker player, and I'd say he could have gone the direction of playing professional if he'd wanted to. He used to play snooker with Dad all the time in this arcade. I'd be playing the arcade game 'Bubble, Bubble' and sometimes when I went over to have a go I'd say to Peter and Dad,

"Can I play?"

Peter would never let me be his partner because I'd just hold him back. So Dad had to let me play with him for a bit. Peter would have been beating Dad big time as it was, but when I was allowed to be Dad's partner for a bit, Peter would go striding even further ahead. Anytime I potted a red, I'd most likely miss the colour. There was one time when I actually potted red, colour, red, but that was extremely rare. Dad was very good to me that way. He'd let me play with him even though he knew he'd just fall even further behind Peter.

Chapter 15

One very wet Sunday we were heading home to Dublin. The roads were very mucky and slippery, and the rain was pouring down. We'd gone past Oulart, which was only about three miles from our house, and were heading up twisty roads towards Monageer.

Suddenly a black car came heading straight for us. The young man who was driving was going far too fast for the weather conditions, aside from the fact that he should have been driving more slowly anyway on the small and twisty back roads. My Dad knew that whatever he did he had to avoid a head-on collision. There was an electric pole a bit further ahead on the left-hand side of the road. On our side of the electric pole, there was a gate into a field with a cement slab in front of it and a ditch on either side of it, just behind the pole.

Amazingly, Dad managed to get the car sitting in the ditch with the cement slab behind the car, and the electric pole to the right of it. If you wanted to put the car in that position you wouldn't be able to. I actually found it quite entertaining. We couldn't get out the two left doors as they were up against the ditch. The back door on the right side of the car was up against the pole, so we couldn't get out that door either. Dad's door wouldn't open because that was where the black car hit us and messed up the door.

I was the first to get out of the car. I really enjoyed opening the window, taking hold of the pole and pulling myself out of the car. Peter followed me out, and the two of us just stood around on the empty road. The black car had gone and left brake marks behind it. The rain had stopped, so at least that was something. After a few minutes, Mum asked me how I got out and I told her about grabbing on to the pole, so she climbed into the back seat of the car and pulled herself out. Dad was just sitting in the front seat trying to stay calm.

Mum, Peter and myself walked up the road a bit to a house. The people who lived there were very good to us. They brought us in and made us a cup of tea, and then went back down to the car and helped Dad to get out by cutting back the hedge. Dad wouldn't have been able to climb out as he was too big. The Gardai came and examined the scene, and we ended up going back to Garryvadden for the night. We got the next day off school, which was great. Mum drove the car back up to Dublin the next day as Dad wasn't up to driving. He was still recovering from the trauma of it all. It was just the driver's door that was bashed in and couldn't be opened, but apart from that the car was fine. Mum and Dad got the car fixed up when we were back in Dublin.

There'd be times during the summer when, weather permitting, we'd go to the beach. As a child, I never found the idea of going to the beach a big thrill at all, but when I got there, I guess I never wanted to leave. The big question every time was what we were going to do when we got there. The weather was never that great, so the chances of getting into the water were rare enough. Once I got into the water though, which usually took quite some time because of the cold Irish sea, I never wanted to get out. I loved the waves. I loved the way they lifted me up and took control of my body in the water. On a few occasions, we bought a kite to bring with us, and although we were never able to get it up in the air, we still had great fun trying. Dad would have got a Frisbee for us sometimes too, but I was never able to spin it very well, although I mastered it later in life.

Sometimes, when some cousins came to stay with us in Garryvadden, Peter and myself would take them over to Bill O'Brien's place across the lane. We'd climb over the metal gate and then into the barn, and have great fun climbing around all the Swiss roll bales of hay. It was great!! One time Peter and myself found two baby hedgehogs in the hay on the ground in front of the barn. This was an amazing experience for us. We told Dad and we asked him if we could keep them. He said "Yes", so we got a cardboard box and we put some hay in it, and then I lifted up one of the hedgehogs from underneath his body and put him into the box. I had no problem lifting him up at all. Their spikes were quite soft and they hadn't learned how to control them yet, so the spikes were kind of sloped backwards so you could nearly stroke them.

We named the hedgehogs Bill and Ben, and we brought them home with us and left them in the box at the back of the house. Then I went and got some worms for them. I threw one or two worms into the box with them. Ben was big enough to eat the worm, and the worm gave him some strength so he was able to escape. He must have climbed up the box and rolled down the other side. At one stage Peter was playing outside, and he saw Ben down inside one of the nine-inch cavity blocks on the foundations of a greenhouse that Dad had got Ian to build onto the side of the shed.

At the time I actually didn't believe Peter had found Ben there—I thought Peter had put him there—but that wouldn't make sense at all. So we had to get him out of the wall, which was about three blocks up from the ground. Ben had got stuck down at least a foot into the wall. What happened then was that I managed to slide my skinny little arm down the hole and get my hand under Ben and pull him back up. I was thrilled with myself. What a success! Then I put him back in the box with Bill but he escaped again and we didn't see him after that.

Poor Bill though, he just kept getting weaker and weaker. We tried to feed him milk but he just wasn't able to take it. After a few days, Bill died and there was nothing we could do about it, so we just brought him behind the shed and dug a hole with the spade and buried him in the ground. I got two sticks and put them on top of the ground in the shape of a cross. Then I just said under my breath 'Goodbye Bill'.

Another aspect of nature that we had in Garryvadden was a family of swallows that made their home in a hole in our roof, just at the corner of the house to the side of the kitchen door. Every year the swallows would come back and build their nest there and raise their chicks. It was lovely.

At some point, maybe a year or two after the shed had been built, Dad got Ian to help him build a yard out at the back of the house and a pathway down the far side of the house. The way that Dad decided to do it was very artistic. First, he got Ian to make two steps up to the back door. Next he got him to build a wall about three feet high going straight out from the back corner of the house, on the side where the shed was. Then, Dad got Ian to leave a gap in the wall and make two steps down to a lower yard in front of the shed.

So we had an upper yard, basically surrounded by walls, and a lower yard. If you were standing in the middle of the upper yard looking out at a beautiful sunset, which we did many a time, the house would be behind you, and our herb wall would be in front of you. Dad got Ian to make his herb wall by building two walls parallel to each other and filling the space between them with soil. Of course he would have built blocks up on each side of the wall as well to keep the soil inside. Then he planted loads of herbs, such as mint, parsley, thyme, sage, chives and a few others. He also planted one or two shrubs there as well.

Chapter 16

Looking back I'd say television wouldn't have been a big aspect of my life, at least until I started school. I always remember having colour television in Dublin. The biggest thing I associate with television when I was small is Betty. It seemed to me that Betty did nothing but watch television and she was getting paid for it. She used to watch the Sullivans, Emmerdale Farm, Sons and Daughters, and God knows what else.

I know I used to love watching Bosco, and I actually remember fighting with Peter over whether Bosco was a boy or a girl. Peter was insistent that Bosco was a girl and I knew that Bosco was a boy. Of course he was both really, the puppet was a boy and it was a woman that did his voice. My favourite part of the programme was story time, which happened after the magic door. I can even remember the rhyme they said before they went through the magic door. "Knock knock open wide, see what's on the other side, knock knock any more, come with me through the magic door". Then one of the two presenters would open the door and next thing we'd see an educational film, which was usually footage of some kind of animal. They would also sing songs and do some kind of make and do, but I liked the story the best.

I watched Sesame Street as well. There were way more puppets in Sesame Street, and there was Big Bird which was either a man or a woman dressed up in a big feathery bird suit which looked great. Some of my favourite puppets in Sesame Street were Bert and Ernie, two brothers that shared a bedroom. Bert was always in bed trying to sleep and Ernie was always pottering around the bedroom making noise and getting on Bert's nerves. I loved Ernie because he looked like so much fun, whereas Bert I didn't like at all because he was always so grumpy.

Elmo was a gorgeous little puppet, so cute. You can still buy him in the shops today. The cookie monster was gas, stuffing his face with cookies and bits of the cookies flying everywhere. I don't know if he said anything or not. I didn't really like Oscar, who lived in a rubbish bin. He was a really dirty puppet if you ask me. I think Sesame Street was on while we were in school so we only got to watch it when we were sick or on holidays. I also watched "Rainbow", which I quite liked, though all I really remember of it were the two puppets "Zippy" and "George". Zippy was a brown puppet with a round head and a zip for his mouth, and "George" was a pink hippopotamus.

The cartoons I loved were "Tom and Jerry", Tom being the blue cat that could never catch "Jerry" the lovely little brown mouse. I loved "Jerry", he was so cute. I also loved "Tweety Pie", the lovely little yellow bird that the cat could never catch either. I'm pretty sure that was what the cartoon was based on, but the main reason I loved this was the fact that Tweety was so cute as well. I loved Donald Duck but I wasn't so keen on Daffy Duck, probably because he was a bit of a grumpy duck. I think the film "Who framed Roger Rabbit" was brilliant the way it brought all of the old cartoons together in a new film. I think it was the first film that actually combined film and animation together. I didn't see it in the cinema but I've watched it many times since.

The first television we had was a big 'Bush' television. When we were in Dublin on Friday nights, the family would come together in the sitting room and watch television together. Dad had his chair in the corner of the room, Mum would be lying out on the couch and Peter and myself would be on the floor. The Late Late show was Friday night's landmark, and probably still is for a lot of Irish householders. I hated having to sit in front of The Late Late show for what seemed like such a long time. Every time there was a break and it would say on the screen 'end of part 1' or another part, I would say to Dad,

"How many more parts are there?"

I don't think he ever answered me.

There was one lovely thing about lying on the floor in the sitting room. There was, and still is, a lovely painting over the fireplace and I used to just gaze into it and drift away to another world. This time it was a lovely calm, peaceful and quiet world as it was a painting of the seashore. There were one or two rocks in the sea, there was a cliff on the right side of the painting and some more rocks on the left. Out in the distance there was an island, and above all of this the moon was hiding behind a cloud and you could see the light of the moon coming out around the cloud. I loved this painting so much, and I would have been staring into it while Gay Byrne was talking to his guests on The Late Late show.

In those days, you had to press the button in on the television to change channels, and Dad would often ask me to go and do this. I don't think I minded it that much though. When the remote control came along, the fights it caused were something else. There were times when Gay Byrne would be giving away a prize to somebody at home of a trip to Disneyland. I'd get all excited and say to Mum and Dad "Can we go to Disneyland?"

Peter and myself never got to go to Disneyland. I'm not sure why though. Mum and Dad probably had better things to spend their money on.

As I said before, when we had Garryvadden first we only had a black and white television with two channels, and I remember one weekend when Mum and Dad brought the huge Bush television down, so we could watch the Eurovision song contest. I loved the Eurovision, and it ended up being a landmark in the year for me. The songs were great, and the result was often quite close which made it really exciting, and there was always the possibility of us winning. Now the way things have gone I don't think we have much of a chance of winning at all. Not because of the talent in Ireland but because of the fact that we're out here on our own, on our lovely little island, and with the tele-voting everyone votes for their neighbours. But I guess you never know with these things. It might happen yet.

The Grand National was another landmark during the year for me. Dad loved watching the horse racing on the television on Saturdays and he'd often put on bets. The Grand National was such a big race that Dad would put on quite a few bets. There were so many horses and I loved the way all the horses were listed in The Irish Times newspaper. I loved looking at the colours the jockeys were going to be wearing, and all the different, interesting names of the horses. I'd sometimes pick certain horses because of their name, or because of the colours the jockey was going to be wearing, and I'd say that I was up for them. Sometimes I won and I got such a thrill, it was great!

I also loved watching the Dublin Horse Show in August. It was, and still is, a sport full of hope. Will he knock the pole off, will he get a clear run? Of course if he was one of the Irish riders, I'd be hoping all the time that he wouldn't knock a pole. But when it came to the horses for the other countries, of course I'd be hoping the opposite for them. 'Please knock a pole', I'd be thinking. I always felt that the length of time it took wasn't that important, if they could just get around the course without faulting it would be great.

I think it's a beautiful and quite artistic sport . . . The way the horses and the jockeys are dressed up and the beautiful way the course is laid out. I particularly loved the water jump. I'll tell you something though, my favourite part of the whole Dublin Horse Show is still the Puissance, where the horses have to jump over a big high wall. If the horse makes it over the wall without knocking one of the bricks he gets to go on to the next round, but if he knocks down a brick then, he's out. After all of the countries have had their go, another brick is put up, and the wall gets higher. The wall just keeps getting higher and higher until none of the horses can jump it. The last horse left is the winner. I think the presentation of the medals and prizes is beautifully done as well.

The other landmark in August was the Rose of Tralee. Dad couldn't stand this programme, so he'd probably stay in the kitchen and read the paper or something, but I used to stay up late and watch it with Mum. The Rose of Tralee was something Mum and myself enjoyed doing together, though I have to say this is another time when I kept my feelings and opinions to myself. Mum would be going on about the ladies' hair and their dresses and so on. I'd be sitting there listening and just taking it all in. I loved the colours, but what I loved most was when each lady did her party piece. I particularly liked it if she was doing a dance. Of course dancing is in my blood on my mum's side of the family. I've always loved dancing. I never had the confidence for it when I was a child, but now I can't get enough of it.

The first time I went to the cinema was when Mum took me to see E.T. I was about five and I can vaguely remember it. I can't remember going to the cinema much as a child, but that might have been because I didn't have any friends to go with. I loved watching films on the television though, and some that I really liked, I watched over and over again. I can remember being down in Dungarvan at the August bank holiday weekend, and after the barbeque Mum, Dad, Peter and myself would go down to Auntie Rose and Uncle Jack's house. Some of our other cousins would sometimes come down as well. Rose was great. She'd put on a video for us to watch, and one of the films she put on was "Annie". I think this might have been the first time I saw it, but I watched Annie over and over again as a child, so many times that I know it off by heart. Other films I watched over and over were "Mary Poppins" and "The Sound of Music". I really loved these particular films and I'd be singing away to them as I was watching, but it can't have been very pleasant for other people who were nearby, as I don't have a note in my head.

Chapter 17

During primary school, there were times when I was taken out of school for procedures to be done to my head, in order to try and get more information about my epilepsy. There were two procedures in particular that I can remember quite clearly. One was where the doctor stuck little metal discs to my head. There were wires connected to the little discs, which I presume must have been connected to some machine. Anyway, when I had these wires connected to me, I had to lie down and stay very still for about half an hour. I had no problem with that at all. I just did what I was told and it was over before I knew it.

The other thing they did was to take photographs of my brain. For this procedure, I was put lying down on a machine, a good bit up off the ground. The machine then slid me all the way inside some sort of dark tunnel, and when my head was in there that's when they took the photographs. This didn't bother me at all either. I just had to lie there and stay very still and be patient. I was so used to being on my own and doing nothing that this was a grand little rest for me. I was told later in life that the photographs of my brain were so perfect that the doctor was able to use them for examples of the brain for student doctors. They couldn't really find anything wrong with my brain, so these seizures that I was having quite regularly were a bit of a mystery.

Anyway, these procedures got me out of school for a while, and I was very happy with that.

I hated Irish or 'Gaeilge', as it was put up on the board. I just couldn't understand it at all, and I couldn't see the point of going to all this trouble to learn it either, particularly when there wasn't going to be any chance of speaking it outside of school. I could get the words okay, but the grammar I found impossible. I couldn't master it at all. Mum wasn't good at Irish either so maybe that's why Irish wouldn't have been one of my strong points . . . That is if I had any strong points at all. I'm sure I never saw them anyway. Although I was pretty good at art, as I mentioned earlier.

I found English very difficult too. I was always so slow at writing, and this probably had to do with confidence and my memory. I was never happy with the way my handwriting looked. It never came close to being as good as Mum's writing, but of course as a teacher, Mum would have had to have good, clear handwriting. Dad's writing was desperate, and I could hardly ever make out what he'd written. My spellings would have held me back as well. I was so bad at spelling, both in Irish and in English. I just could never remember how to spell the words at all, and I never had the confidence for it anyway. Though there were a couple of times that I wrote essays, with Mum's encouragement, and I got an excellent for both of them.

I was no good at Maths either. I found the times tables very hard to learn and I couldn't see the point of it either. I just hated school overall, and I couldn't wait for when I grew up and I could do what I wanted. Mum was great with my education though. One summer, when we were down in Wexford, I was having a lot of trouble with my seven times tables. Mum cut out twelve big rectangular pieces of paper, and on each piece of paper she wrote one of the twelve multiples of seven. Then she stuck them up in different areas in the house. Some that I remember clearly are the ones that she stuck on the toilet cistern, and another one that she stuck on one of the wardrobes. I had particular trouble with seven multiplied by seven, and six multiplied by seven, but Mum's system was great. She'd ask me one of the multiplications, and if I didn't know the answer I was allowed to run to the place in the house where the answer was, and run back to Mum and tell her.

The fact that Mum never liked history rubbed off on me big time so I ended up hating history. I really enjoyed learning about the wooden horse of Troy though, probably because I was able to link it with something I already knew about. Actually I didn't find history too bad in primary school. I don't think I liked Geography at all. I found it so hard to learn all the counties of Ireland. I managed to learn off all the counties of Ulster very well, but that's about as far as I got.

Another subject I couldn't take in was religion. I don't think I got any of my connections with religion from school. Any, or maybe even all, of my religious beliefs and feelings I would have got through family, neighbours and experiences. There were some things about religion that I loved in primary school though. I loved going to Mass with the school on days like Ash Wednesday, for example, because I was one of the group. I loved having the ashes on my forehead because it made me feel noticed. It made me feel there was a reason to be alive, a reason to be someone, to be there with everyone else. The ashes united me with all the other children. I also loved all the times we spent time working on decorations for the church for special occasions, like First Confession or first Holy Communion. That was probably because of my great love for art.

It always felt good to realise we were coming to the end of the school day, but there were also things about it that I didn't like, homework for instance. We had to take down our homework off the board and write it into our journals. I was so slow at writing that it seemed to take forever before I actually managed to get it all down off the board. Not only did I have the awful pain of writing, but I also had all this work on my shoulders that I knew I was going to have to struggle through for what seemed like an eternity when I got home.

First, of course, I had to go through the walk home with the horrible weight of my very heavy bag full of books on my shoulders. When Aisling was away in the Middle East it was even worse, because I had to do it all on my own. I don't know how long it actually took me to get home, but with my little legs and my very heavy bag I'd say it took about twenty minutes. I was the miserable little girl walking along the footpath with my bag sliding down my arms, and my head down looking straight into the never-ending footpath in front of me.

When I did finally get home, it was to an empty house. I don't know if Peter was even there the whole time. I can remember looking out the sitting room window, waiting for Mum to come home. I don't know what happened about food for us when we had to wait by ourselves in the house for an hour until Mum got home. Although I clearly remember the time that Peter and myself sneaked two Petit Filous out of the fridge. The two of us were eating our Petit Filous when we heard Mum coming in the front door. I'm not sure what I did with mine, but I saw Peter digging his teaspoon into the little tub, and basically pulling the whole yogurt out of the tub, shoving it in his mouth and gulping it down in one go, just leaving the pot and the spoon on the counter. I was there thinking what a waste it was. When I'd be eating a Petit Filous, I'd savour every last spoonful, and I'd scrape the tub very thoroughly until there was nothing left.

I remember an incident that happened when I was walking home from school one day. This girl, whose name I knew was Vanessa, although I don't think she was in my class, was walking home in front of me. Suddenly, she turned around and said to me,

"What are you looking at?"

This upset me a little bit, because I wasn't even looking at her. I was probably looking down at the path as usual, but I basically just tried to forget about it and walked on.

Another day when I was walking home Vanessa came up to me with a little carton of orange juice and started pouring the orange juice all over my hair. I did nothing and just kept walking, but Vanessa followed me and kept saying "sticky sticky orange", as she kept pouring it over me until it was all gone. Luckily this happened in June, and Mum was there when I got home. I was very upset and if Mum hadn't been there, it would have been a disaster, but she was thank God. Mum took care of me and washed my hair, and talked to me about Vanessa, basically trying to give some reason for her awfully mean behaviour. I don't remember any other trouble from Vanessa, so it was probably just an isolated incident.

One day in June when I got home from school, Mum told me that my grandma had been in a car accident. I got a fright when I heard this but I can remember doing a drawing especially for my grandma while she was going through this awful time. She was an amazing woman. She'd been crossing the road and got hit by a car. She was actually thrown up in the air and landed on the bonnet of the car. Her right shoulder and hip were badly injured and she had to have metal put in to help the bones merge back together. After the surgery, she was in a wheelchair at first but after a while she had crutches. Mum told me that she was in tears as she was going through the physiotherapy to help her walk again, but she got through it all and made a full recovery.

Chapter 18

My grandparents used to come down to Garryvadden quite regularly. I know that the first time they came down Mum and Dad gave them the double bed that they'd got from Aunt Rose and Uncle Jack, and the four of us must have slept on airbeds or something. In their own house, my grandparents had their own separate beds, so I couldn't believe that they could actually sleep in a double bed together. It didn't seem right at all.

Sometimes when they stayed with us, we'd all go out together for dinner and Grandpa would treat us to a nice meal. We used to go to Kelly's hotel in Rosslare, and when Peter and myself had finished eating and were getting restless, we could go to a crazy golf course outside where they could all look out at us playing. Peter was always so much better at it than me but I never stopped trying to be as good at it as he was.

One time, just after the six of us arrived back to the house in Garryvadden, my grandpa fell backwards down off the big step into the house. Amazingly, all that happened to him was a bit of a graze on his head. I got an awful fright and I was nearly crying. It's one of the nicest memories I have of my grandpa, because I actually don't know him that well, but I can remember him reassuring me that he was alright. He said to me

"Your grandpa is as tough as old boots".

He surely was. I can remember him telling me that he'd never been in hospital. He used to show us his baby finger that was bent down and that he wasn't able to lift. He told us that he could get something cut inside his hand to straighten it out, but he couldn't be bothered. He really hated hospitals. Another thing that was unusual about my grandpa was that he had no sense of smell. He was never able to smell from the day he was born.

When they came down to visit us, my grandparents would take the train, as they had free travel. One time, when Grandma was walking along inside the train looking for a seat, she tripped and fell. My poor grandma, she ended up injuring the other side of her body this time . . . her left shoulder and her left hip. The train was delayed for quite some time as we waited for an ambulance. Then Grandpa went with Grandma in the ambulance, and the four of us followed them in the car all the way to Dublin. Grandpa told us afterwards that the driver was very good. He drove slowly and carefully, to make the journey as smooth as possible so as not to cause my grandma any more pain or discomfort.

One thing I liked about travelling back to Dublin on a Sunday afternoon was that when we reached Bunclody, which was the first main town on our way home, Dad would pull in somewhere and park the car. We'd get out and go into one particular newsagent to buy ice-cream cones. It was the most gorgeous ice cream and all four of us would have one each.

Another part of the Sunday journey that I liked was the bit towards the end, when we were going over the Wicklow Mountains. I remember looking at the vast amount of pure green grass all around us. There was really nothing in sight, just beautiful green grass, and we were driving along on a little road in the middle of it. Even though there were no trees, flowers, houses, birds or any creatures to be seen, I still found it absolutely beautiful. I also knew that when we got to this area we were nearly home. This area was also beautiful in spring, when you'd see newborn lambs and sheep on either side of the road. I used to be looking out the window very intently to see if I could spot a black lamb. Once or twice I actually saw one, and it was so special because black lambs are quite unusual.

In the autumn, the evenings were gradually getting darker as we were travelling home from Wexford. Now I would have slept through a lot of it, but when I woke up towards the end of the journey and saw that we were going over the Wicklow Mountains, I'd become quite alert for a girl who suffered from carsickness. As you're coming towards County Dublin from the Wicklow Mountains in the dark, you have the most fabulous view . . . All the golden yellow lights of Dublin down below you. It was gorgeous.

It was a bit like being on a plane. Although I'd never been on a plane when I was this age, the reason I knew that was because of something Mum used to say when we reached this part of our journey.

"Ladies and Gentlemen, we are now coming into Dublin airport. Please fasten all seatbelts and extinguish all cigarettes and no smoking until we reach the terminal building."

I loved this and as soon as I saw the lights I'd say to Mum,

"Say the line, say the line". I thought it was great!

Then when we finally reached our lovely estate I was delighted. When we were small, and particularly in the spring, we'd probably get some time to run around with some of the other children on the road before dinner.

There were quite a few houses with children around the same age as Peter and myself, which was great. Two doors down from us there were the Keeleys, who had four children, three boys and a girl. Next door there was Aisling and her twin sisters. Our other next door neighbours were the McMullans, and they had four children as well. I can remember Mum and Dad commenting on this family, and in particular being impressed by their birth control, the way they had the four children spaced with around five years between each baby. They were also blessed with two boys and two girls.

When I heard this I kind of thought to myself, that's the number of children I'd like to have. All I really wanted was to be surrounded by children and babies. I just loved them so much. I think a big part of this was because little children don't judge you. They just take you as you are and they're so full of love. I wanted babies so much, but when I thought about my epilepsy and how that could affect my ability to look after small children, it used to get me down. If I was having seizures, which were only getting more regular, how was I going to be able to take care of a tiny helpless baby?

There was a family of four with two boys beside the McMullans, and the younger boy was in Peter's class. Across the road there were the Logans, Fiona and Alan, who had the biggest family on the road. Fiona became Mum's closest friend, probably because they both loved gardening. Fiona and Alan's children were all boys. Sadly, their sixth boy, Niall ended up dying a cot death before his first birthday. Fiona decided that the best way to get over losing her lovely baby boy was to get pregnant again. Nine months later Fiona gave birth to unexpected twins, first a boy and then a girl. We were all delighted for them, now Fiona and Alan had a daughter, such a lovely surprise. It was great!!

Next to the Logans there was another family of four with a boy and a girl, just like our family. I was delighted when the Hannons (who I told you about bullying me earlier) moved away, and a lovely family with four more children moved into their house. The eldest girl, Paula was quite friendly with me and I spent a lot of time with this family. They also had a fifth baby after they moved in, a lovely baby boy. Paula was thrilled that they were the second biggest family on the road. Unfortunately, even though I was friends with Paula, I'd never learned to open up to anyone. I could never tell anyone my feelings and I was still very quiet.

There were the Flanagans, who lived next door to Paula. They had two boys and a girl but I don't think I saw too much of them around that time. There really was quite a shortage of girls on our road. At one stage, a girl named Saoirse had joined the road but no one was approaching her to welcome her and invite her over to play with the rest of us. There were times when I'd feel inside of me that I should go over to her and talk to her, but I wasn't a leader. I just followed what everyone else did. I didn't have the motivation or the confidence to do it, but I kind of felt guilty that I didn't. Aisling didn't seem to have any interest in approaching Saoirse at all. Eventually Fiona, a girl from the house on the corner of the main road, approached Saoirse and invited her into the group. I thought to myself, fair play to Fiona, it's about time Saoirse joined in with the rest of us.

Saoirse, Aisling and myself formed our own little group after that, but I was so quiet that I guess it was natural that Saoirse became better friends with Aisling than with me. I always fancied Alan throughout all the years we'd grown up together. Alan was one of the Logan boys from across the road and he was around the same age as Aisling, Saoirse and myself, but Alan had his eye on Aisling. I found that a bit annoying, because Aisling never seemed to be interested in Alan, but I guess that's life. Over time I ended up being pushed out of the group. Saoirse and Aisling had lost interest in me altogether and so I was left with no friends at all.

Anyway, I was saying that I was delighted to be home in Dublin again. Dinner on a Sunday evening was always steak, because it was nice and quick to cook. I loved this dinner—steak, chips, mushrooms and lovely fried onions—and it would set me up nicely for bed pretty soon after.

Chapter 19

Now I was in fourth class and my epilepsy was still haunting me. I had no idea when it was going to come over me again but I knew it was going to happen at some stage, which was a horrible, depressing and uncomfortable feeling. My teacher's name was Mrs. Pepper. I quite liked her as I felt she was a good teacher and was able to discipline the class very well. There were a lot of rowdy boys in my class, which I didn't like at all particularly being a teacher's daughter and a teacher's pet.

One thing I remember very clearly about fourth class is that at about two o'clock each day, half an hour before home time, Mrs. Pepper would read to us. One of the girls in the class had brought in a beautiful hardback copy of Matilda by Roald Dahl, and Mrs. Pepper read some of it to us every day. I had never experienced anything like it before, and I really loved it. I don't remember much else about that school year, but I'm sure I was still finding the schoolwork very difficult and was still getting loads of support from Mum when it came to homework later on in the day.

It was around this time that I got my 'facts of life' talk from Mum. One day, Mum came home from school with a small package. She brought me up to my bedroom and sat me down beside her on my bed. She opened up the box and what she took out of it was a small box of Tampax, a plastic container to hold tampons and a little booklet. Mum went through the booklet very thoroughly with me, and she told me about all the changes that were going to happen to my body, which I wasn't happy with at all. I always wanted to be a boy and do all the things a boy could do and this was just going to make things worse.

Mum explained very clearly how the tampons worked. Then she talked to me about the love between a man and a woman. There were illustrations in the booklet of the changes in a man's body and the changes in a woman's body. When Mum explained to me about making love with a man she told me that it was something very special, and she also said it could actually be quite painful. I asked Mum how many men she'd slept with, and she told me that the only man she had slept with was Dad. The idea of this kind of touched my heart and it seemed really special, so at that very moment I decided that I only wanted one man and I thought that maybe I'd even wait until my wedding night to make love with my one man in a lovely bed in a really expensive room in the hotel where we had our wedding reception.

After hearing about who Mum had slept with, I got curious about Dad, so one evening when he was down on his knees lighting the fire I said to him,

"Dad, did you ever sleep with anyone other than Mum?"

Dad's reply to me was "Shhh".

I thought to myself well fair enough, if you don't want to talk about it that's okay with me and I left the room.

At one stage around this time I got very upset about my body changing. I can actually remember lying on my bed crying because of it. Mum came over to comfort me and she said,

"Well, we get to feel what it's like to have a baby grow inside us".

I was okay after that, because I already wanted to be around babies and children so much. But this made me want a baby even more and I couldn't see how that could possibly happen, since I had epilepsy, which definitely wasn't getting any better.

I was in fifth class now and my new teacher was Mr. Wood. Of all my teachers in primary school, he was my favourite. When the principal came into the class at the end of the year and told us that we were having Mr. Wood again for sixth class, I was delighted, though I did think to myself that the other pupils in the class wouldn't have been at all as happy as I was. As you know, I was really bad at spelling, so one of the things I liked about Mr. Wood was that he used to call out our spellings in the mornings, and do Maths Challenge with us as well, without correcting them so I didn't feel so bad.

Sometimes I used to imagine myself as the teacher in the classroom. Maybe it was because I have teacher's blood in me, from my mum, my grandma, and you could say my dad as well, as he ran courses for young adults. I used to think about the way I'd lay out the desks in order to keep the boys from messing, and I used to imagine what it would be like to call the roll.

Around this time I mentioned to Mum that I was thinking about getting my hair cut, and wondering whether people might think I was a boy. Dad used to cut Peter's hair, and when I was younger I'd asked my dad to cut my hair short and that was a disaster, as loads of people thought I was a boy. Mum said that the fact that my body was changing and I was getting curves meant that people would be more aware that I was a girl. So I got my hair cut in the hairdressers when Mum was having hers cut. I didn't have the confidence to choose the kind of hairstyle I wanted, so Mum talked to the hairdresser and she basically gave me the same sort of cut that Mum had.

I never really liked the way the hairdresser styled my hair, but it was much easier to manage so I kept it like that for all of sixth class. I even had my hair short for my Confirmation. Bishop Ian Freedman confirmed me and I chose the name May for it. I would have spent quite some time working on decorations for the church during this year in school. We cut out letters for the seven gifts we'd be getting e.g. WISDOM. I think we cut out little flames as well and we each had to bring in a photo for our own flame, all of which would be stuck up beautifully on the church wall.

I'd been spending a fair amount of time with a girl called Amy. Even though I wasn't opening up to her that much, I was still hanging around with her. Once or twice, I went back to her house after school, quite reluctantly, as I was in such a routine of going straight home and waiting for Mum that it didn't feel right going anywhere without Mum knowing. I can remember being given toasted cheese sandwiches when I went to Amy's house, which was lovely.

Now that I was in sixth class it was time to start thinking about secondary school. I had mentioned to Mum a year or two previously that I wanted to go to Sancta Maria College. The reason I chose that college was because I liked the wine colour of the uniform. At some stage in sixth class I asked Amy what secondary school she was going to. When she said that she was going to Our Lady's College, I was very disappointed, because at this stage it was too late for me to change my mind and go there too, which was what I really wanted. Our Lady's would probably have suited better socially because a lot of the girls in Sancta Maria lived a good distance away. I would also get the impression that the discipline would be better. The nuns were far too easy going, they never reinforced the rules, like they let the girls wear a different style of uniform than had been chosen for them which really made me stand out as different because I always wore the correct uniform but I guess that's the way life goes sometimes.

There was one day in sixth class that I don't think I'll ever forget, because it felt so good. Towards the end of the school day one of the boys in the class came up to me at my table and said to me,

"Do you want to go out with me?"

I said "No".

I mean I'd been in this class for nearly eight years, and only one or two pupils in the class had ever said anything to me at all throughout all that time. Most of the pupils had never even approached me during the whole of primary school. So I was hardly just going to say "Yes" straight away to someone I hardly knew.

Although that's similar to the situation I'm in with Alex at the moment. Things seem to be getting quite serious between Alex and myself and I don't know an awful lot about him. But I do know more about him than I did about the boys in primary school, and what Alex and myself have is very special so I guess it's actually quite a different situation.

Anyway, after that boy had left me and gone back to his seat, another boy in the class came up to me and asked me exactly the same question. I said "No" for the same reason I'd said "No" to the previous boy. This routine went on for quite some time as nearly all of the boys in the class asked me to go out with them. While I was enjoying rejecting all of the boys, one of the girls who was sitting at the table I was at said to me,

"Sarah, you are so lucky".

I didn't reply to this comment but I thought to myself, I'm lucky . . . well which would you prefer? To be able to choose whatever boy you wanted and have to suffer on your own and go through life with epilepsy, or to be perfectly healthy and happy without a boy.

I was now at the age when I was allowed to sit in the front seat of the car and I can still remember it very clearly. I was sitting in the front seat with Mum beside me, and I was all excited and delighted to be sitting in the front of the car. Then Mum said to me,

"Put on your seat belt".

I said "No".

Mum said "If you don't put on your seat belt I'm not moving".

She didn't move so I put it on, and from that day forward, I'd never take a lift in the front seat of a car without putting on my seatbelt.

As secondary school was approaching, it was time to think about what subjects to choose. Well, I was definitely going to choose

French, as Mum was a French teacher and could give me loads of help. The other choice was Spanish. Then there was the choice between science and home economics. I found this choice quite difficult because I wanted to experience both of them. I asked Mum which of the two subjects I should choose and she said,

"Well, you could do science and I'll teach you home economics".

In the end I chose science, but now I think I would have been better off choosing home economics, but I guess that's the way life goes sometimes.

Chapter 20

It was about this time in my life that a new family moved into our estate. Susan and Philip Robertson moved into a house up at the other end of the road on the same side as our house. They had a baby girl named Katie and she was about six months old at the time. I spent a lot of time pushing Katie in her buggy, up and down the footpath in the estate. I had quite a lot of contact with this new family and I watched it grow as time went on. As Susan had more babies, I helped her to feed them and I played with them too. I was in my element spending time with her young family as I loved children so much. As well as having children myself, I'd actually have liked to work with children, but that wasn't on the cards because of my epilepsy, which was showing no signs of improving.

I ended up in Sancta Maria College and I started growing my hair again. I made hardly any friends at all while I was in secondary school. Maybe one, but it wouldn't have been a very close friendship at all.

I got used to having more than one teacher very quickly and I didn't mind it at all. I don't know how I felt about having free classes though. I suppose I quite liked it but I'd still have kept to myself for most of it. As time went on, although probably not in first year, I developed more confidence in doing my homework myself, and then I really valued the free classes for getting my homework done.

My epilepsy was just getting worse. I was having seizures nearly every month, which meant that I was missing a lot of school. I don't think I actually had many seizures in school though. What happened was that I'd have a seizure at night in bed, and then Mum and Dad would keep me home from school. It was horrible. After having the seizure in bed, we all knew that I was going to have at least one more seizure, but it was usually two or three more. I'd have them while I was lying on the couch watching a film on the television that I was hardly able to follow at all.

I'd have the scary aura following me everywhere as well, and I wouldn't come back to being myself for a whole week. I would have slept an awful lot too. This aura was a horrible shadow that followed me everywhere. It was a very unpleasant feeling . . . It was the feeling I used to get before I'd have a seizure, but now I was getting it after I had a seizure as well and the feeling would last the whole week. The aura was just as bad as, if not worse than, the seizure itself. I'm not sure what doctor I was under for my epilepsy at that stage, but whoever he was and whatever medications he had me on, they weren't doing much good. My epilepsy was still ruining my life and there was nothing I could do about it. I was still trapped in this awful nightmare, and trying to hope for anything in life was just getting harder and harder.

Mum was constantly getting me to pray to the Lord to cure my epilepsy. We'd light candles under the statue of Our Lady in the church. Mum would also be telling me that Our Lady is the one to pray to when you're looking to find a nice man to spend your life with. She'd get me to pray to St. Therese as well, and there was one day that I'll never forget because what happened was so unexpected. Mum and myself went over to the statue of St. Therese in our local church and we lit every candle under the statue and offered it up to cure me of my epilepsy. Then there was Padre Pio. He was the other saint I was told to pray to.

One time there was a family gathering in Aunt Marie's house and my aunt Michelle, that's one of my dad's sisters-in-law, who was big into Padre Pio, gave me a beautiful set of Padre Pio rosary beads. These rosary beads had been in Michelle's family for years, and I could see that it was very hard for her to part with them, but being the very loving woman that she is she gave them to me. They did make some kind of a difference to my epilepsy for a certain amount of time, but unfortunately the seizures came back after about three months.

One day in first year, at the end of a speech and drama class just as we were all leaving the classroom, the teacher called me back and said to me,

"Sarah, hold your head up".

I was a bit taken aback by this so I held my head up as high as it would go and said,

"Like this?"

The speech and drama teacher said "Yes".

From that day on my confidence began to grow.

I never really learned to mix with any of the girls, so I never learnt to do girlie things like shopping for clothes or shoes for example. When I did go shopping it would have been with Mum, and it always seemed like a chore so I never really enjoyed it. I never had the confidence to buy something because I liked it. I'd always ask Mum what she thought, and if she liked it as well then I'd get it.

I'd never gone out drinking either, and I wouldn't even have known that that's what some of the girls in my school, and other schools for that matter, spent their free time doing. I've never been drunk, and all through my teen years the only person I ever saw drunk was my dad, and that wasn't very pleasant at all. But even though my dad took to the drink over the years, he never laid a finger on any of us.

I never had any proper birthday parties through my teen years. The four of us would just have a nice family meal together. I didn't get many presents for my birthdays either. At one stage, Peter and myself used to always get a present of a board game for our birthdays, and I suppose for Christmas as well, and we ended up with a huge collection of board games on the shelves in our playroom. The only problem was that because I had no friends the only people I ever played them with were my family.

At lunch time in school, once I'd finished eating my lunch, I used to walk around the school corridors by myself looking at all the pictures on the walls, and in particular at a picture of Our Lady. I now have a picture of Our Lady myself on my bedroom wall and I look straight at it while lying in bed. So I'd gone from walking around the schoolyard to walking the school corridors. I was still all on my own, but at least now I was out of the cold.

I was still finding the schoolwork very hard, and I pretty much hated every subject except art, which I still loved. Art was mainly focused on what we did in class, so there wouldn't have been much homework involved, not in first year anyway. The homework routine was still there though. When I got home I might have something to eat, then when Mum came home which was very soon after me or sometimes before me, we'd go upstairs and we'd start on my homework.

It was horrible . . . another miserable, lonely day at school and then home to my little box room with Mum to study. I had been sharing the big bedroom with Peter, but as I reached puberty first, well, I guess I needed my own space, so I moved out of the big room and into the box room. This caused quite a few arguments as the years went on.

I can remember learning how to do lino print in art classes, and for my Junior Cert I did a lino print of a chimpanzee in brown. The other three things I did in art for my junior cert were a poster with the theme of the toucan bird, a fabulous embroidery of the toucan, and a puppet of the toucan. For the embroidery, I used a lot of different types of material and different coloured threads and a button for the eye. I had a bit of black feather for the top of his head, and I used a lot of different types of stitches that I'd learnt from a folder called "Embroidery Magic" that I'd asked Mum to get in the shops, and magazines that went with it over a number of weeks. I can still remember my embroidery being put up on display on the wall outside the classroom. I think that in my teen years I was given more of what I asked for, because Mum and Dad would have had more money by then. Though the problem with things like "Embroidery Magic" was how long would I keep it up? Was it a waste of money? So now I feel guilty if I buy something that I end up not using or that I never wear.

When I was making the toucan puppet, I moulded the beak out of pottery and I painted it the different colours. Then I joined the two pieces of pottery together with little bits of wire. I used black furry material for the body, with yellow material for his chest. I made the claws with wire and some kind of stuffing to plump them up, and covered them with blue material. Mrs. Hughes was my teacher's name and when I showed her the puppet she held it up and said to the class,

"Look everybody, look".

Art classes in secondary school weren't just about art, we had to learn about the history of art as well. I wasn't too keen on that because I never liked history very much. Although learning about the history of art actually turned out well in the end, because I got to experience it firsthand when the four of us went on a holiday to Italy. We brought the car with us on the ferry from Rosslare over to France, and then Dad drove all the way through France and through the Alps down to Florence. I would have spent most of the journey lying down in the back of the car because of my carsickness, and I think I had quite a few seizures as well because of the heat. The heat tends to bring on seizures for some reason. Anyway, because I was sick throughout the journey I never got to experience the lovely scenery, but sure I've learned to live with losing out on opportunities due to my epilepsy and carsickness over the years.

When we got to Florence we stayed at a lovely campsite run by a company called Keycamp holidays. The tents were high quality, with fold-up beds, electricity and a fridge. There was a swimming pool in the campsite and I still think that to this day, Mum has never forgiven herself for letting Peter go straight down to the pool without his back covered, because he got sunstroke and was very sick on the first night. But he recovered quite quickly and was back in the pool again in no time.

Peter and myself had a lot of fun in the pool, but there was also an amazing slide at the other end of the campsite and it was huge. There was a massive ladder that you had to climb up. I'd say it was about 18-20 feet high. The slide was yellow and it wasn't just the width of one slide, it was like four slides one beside the other so four people could slide down it at the same time. And it wasn't just a normal slide either. There were four sections in each slide, from top to bottom, with a bump or a ramp between each section. When you got to the end of the slide you went splash into a small but deep rectangular pool of water. It was great!! I don't know how many times we went down it, but it was an awful lot anyway.

While we were in Florence we went to see Brunelleschi's dome, a fabulous piece of architecture. The construction of this dome was nothing short of a miracle. Using ingenious construction techniques and truly innovative engineering concepts, Filippo Brunelleschi, the dome's designer, created a Renaissance masterpiece. We also saw Michelangelo's David, a seventeen foot high marble statue of the biblical hero David. Pisa wasn't very far away so we drove there to see the Leaning Tower of Pisa. I have to say that seeing the Leaning Tower firsthand is a must. It's nothing like the photos.

The other thing we found interesting about Italy was an unusual three-wheeled vehicle. It looked kind of like a van, and there were a few different designs and loads of different colours. The name written on the registration plate was Ape, so we called all these amusing little vehicles "Apes".

Chapter 21

One thing I didn't like about Sancta Maria was the fact that the teachers and the principal, who happened to be a nun, weren't very strict at all and they never reinforced the rules. I was still the goody two shoes of a student and I always did what I was told and followed the rules as best I could. The other girls in the class, and probably in other classes too, didn't wear the correct uniform. I missed loads of PE classes because the girls didn't bring in their PE gear. I loved sport but the girls in my class didn't seem to be too interested in it.

Football was a big part of my life when I was a teenager. I used to play it at home and at school. I really loved it. I've probably mentioned earlier in the book that when I was younger I used to kick a football around with Dad and Peter. I really took to the game "kerbs" as well, which we could only play at the estate in Dublin. This game involved two players, a football and a cul-de-sac road with kerbs on both sides. The objective was to throw the football and try to hit it off the other player's kerb and get the ball to bounce back to you. I was pretty bad at this game but that was probably because I never got much practice at it, except with Peter.

I probably played football with cousins in Garryvadden as well, but what I loved most of all was joining in with the lads on the estate in Dublin. There were three lads on the road the same age as me Alan, Harry and Joseph. They used to get their friends from school to come around to our estate and they'd play football around the corner on the green area. I remember being upstairs in that little room studying with Mum and I'd hear the lads outside on the road. When I heard their voices I'd beg Mum,

"Please can I go out and play with them?"

And she'd pretty well always let me go out.

I'd change into my old jeans and go out to play football with them, although I'd probably hardly say a word to them. We'd head around the corner to the green area and the lads would make two sets of goals with their jackets. Then they'd pick their teams and I'd end up being one of the goalies. That's why I'd wear my old jeans because I'd be diving on the ground a lot and saving goals, which I loved, and every time I dived on to the football the lads would cheer and shout my name.

I was on the school soccer team as well, but I guess the girls didn't really like soccer that much because when I'd go down to the pitch for soccer training there'd only be about three other girls there. I don't know how we actually managed to play against other schools, although we did, but we never won anything.

One time when we were playing against another school, I got injured while I was playing in defence. The football was up in the air and I was looking straight up at it focusing totally on the ball and nothing else, but another girl on the opposite team was doing the exact same thing, and when the ball got to a level where I could head it, the other girl and myself banged heads. I can kind of remember her falling backwards but I was quite disorientated myself. I was stumbling around the side of the pitch with my hand on my head. The coach called me from the other side of the pitch and I went over to him. He spent quite some time putting ice on my head and he said,

"You should have seen the other girl".

I had a nice shiner the following day and I kept repeating the story to everyone who asked how I got it, which I really enjoyed.

I injured myself quite badly a number of times because of my epilepsy. Every time I'd have a seizure I'd chew up my tongue pretty badly, so I'd keep a tube of Bonjela beside my bed to give me some sort of comfort. Now that wasn't actually one of the bad injuries but it was very unpleasant all the same.

Over the years I had three pretty bad injuries, two of which were to my head, the other was to my right arm. One night when I was in bed I had a seizure, and my arm ended up sitting on the boiling hot radiator beside my bed while I was unconscious, and getting very badly burnt. I can remember coming downstairs to Mum and Dad whimpering and holding out my arm to show them how badly I'd burned it. Mum took care of my arm and I was fine and got away without any scars thank God.

Another time I was in Mum and Dad's en suite when I had a seizure and I got my head caught under the radiator and gave myself a very bad black eye, but at least my eyesight wasn't affected. I got another black eye when I had a seizure in bed in Garryvadden, and I kept banging my head off the chest of drawers that was right beside my bed. I gave myself a very bad shiner and my eye was a bit bloodshot for quite some time.

My epilepsy just wouldn't leave me alone. My teen years really consisted of me and my epilepsy, and study, study, study. When I look back on my time in secondary school, I see the two landmarks of Junior Cert and Leaving Cert. I know that I repeated fifth year, which I hated, and I don't think I even understood what my mum was trying to get me through.

I used to cycle to school in the morning but I couldn't do it in one go as it was very hilly. I'd cycle, then walk, and repeat that sequence a few times and eventually I'd get to school. Even though I found the cycle to school hard, I guess I did it because I so much enjoyed cycling home in the evening because I'd fly down the hill and it felt very good.

One of the things I hated in school was taking down notes off the board. The teacher I had for geography was known to the students as Mr. A. He was a very dedicated teacher, and all he did in any of our classes was write tons of information on the blackboard. We had to write all these notes down, and I guess I felt like one of the crowd in this class, but I never really looked at the notes. My hand would be killing me as I was writing and I'd feel like I was behind everybody else. When I got home Mum would take over my study and she'd have her own routine, which never included Mr. A's notes. It felt awful and so pointless putting such effort into taking down these notes and never using them. Our science teacher, Mrs. McNabb was so boring that I used to just sit there staring into space while she was lecturing away to us.

I was still being dragged down to Garryvadden every weekend. The fact that I wasn't in full health with my epilepsy, and that I had no friends, meant that it wasn't safe or logical for me to stay in Dublin. I'd say though that when Peter reached his teen years he was probably allowed to stay in Dublin, for the weekends anyway.

The film I watched a lot in my teens was Dirty Dancing, but I never would have dreamt that I'd be in a real Dirty Dancing kind of scene like I am now. We still had to mow the lawn, which was a huge drag but I guess it had to be done. There was now a big lawn at the back of the house as well. It wasn't as good as the front or side lawns, as it hadn't been levelled since Mum and Dad bought the place, but I have to say that it still looked lovely when it was mowed.

I'd say that at this stage, Dad had built on a greenhouse to the side of the shed. I mentioned earlier that when Ian was building the shed he laid an area of cement beside it and built a three-block wall around it. For many years that area which we called "the lean-to" was used as a kind of dump, and a lot of wood and other things were just thrown into it. When it came to converting this area from "the lean-to" into a greenhouse, we had to clear all the rubbish out of it. Most of it was wood so we had a huge bonfire. We had a good number of bonfires in Garryvadden over the years, usually when we had visitors down with us. We'd have them late in the evening as the sun set, and I have to say that these bonfires were a very enjoyable part of our time in Garryvadden.

After clearing out the "lean-to", Ian and Dad built the greenhouse together using wooden stakes and plenty of glass. They used plastic corrugated sheets for the roof. When the greenhouse was finished, Dad filled in the shed side of it with soil, and put bricks to keep it together. Then he planted lots of tomato plants and cucumbers, courgettes and peppers. So between the vegetable patch up the other side of the house, and the vegetables that we grew in the greenhouse, we had a great selection of vegetables altogether.

Peter and myself were always on the lookout for pets and animals around the place. Quite a number of times we noticed a carrying pigeon outside in the yard with the yellow ring on its foot, obviously taking a break on its flight. We loved looking at it through the kitchen window, and we'd feed it some bread to build up its strength. There was also a wild cat that we called 'Snowy', and he visited us a lot. We used to give him milk, but because he was wild we weren't allowed to pet him, which was a bit disappointing for me anyway. Snowy used to come along with new injuries to his neck nearly every week. He'd have been in fights with other cats and would have been bitten a number of times.

Another incident that happened in Garryvadden as a result of my epilepsy was a very unpleasant seizure, or you could say that what happened after the seizure was the most unpleasant part. What happened was that I was in the shower and I felt a seizure coming on, so I got out of the shower in the thirty seconds warning I'd get beforehand and opened the lock on the bathroom door. The next thing I knew I was standing in the bathroom totally naked with Mum, Dad and Peter just standing there staring at me. It wasn't that long after I had reached puberty, so I would have been quite unsure of my body and the recent changes to it, and I wasn't confident at all. I can remember screaming at the three of them and one of them handing me a towel but that's about it. It was really quite an unpleasant experience.

Peter and myself went through a phase of horse riding for a while, at a place about halfway between Garryvadden and Blackwater. There used to be about three or four other children there as well. We went there quite a few times, but we just barely got to the trotting stage and we were never taken out on walks, which I would have loved. We spent all of our lessons walking, or the odd time trotting, around the paddock.

Over the years there were horses kept in fields around Garryvadden. In the early days, Sean Walsh, who lived at the top of the lane, had let somebody keep their lovely dark brown mare on his land. I remember being told that she was pregnant. She gave birth to a lovely dark brown foal and the two horses were up on Sean's land for quite some time.

Sean was a fascinating man full of interesting stories. His wife was dead at this stage and I can actually still remember her funeral, maybe because it was the first funeral I went to. I can still remember saying to Dad,

"This woman has died, why are we celebrating?"

My dad said,

"Well, when you lose someone you love it's good to have people around you to cheer you up".

I can also remember the way Sean told us that she'd died.

"She's up in heaven now", is what he said.

Minnie was buried in Blackwater with her family, and Sean was left alone in their little cottage with his dog Darky for company. Sean didn't have any teeth and he used to love chewing garlic. At some stage, Sean's dog died and I remember when we came down one weekend he said,

"I buried my dog today".

When Sean died he was buried with his own family in Oulart, the little village on the other side of Garryvadden. Sean and Minnie had a very difficult life. Sean wasn't good to Minnie and he went out drinking a lot, so they ended up being buried with their families and not with each other, which I find quite sad really.

After a few years, the horses were moved down the hill to an area of land near the bridge where we'd often have fun fishing for tiny little fish. I asked Dad for a horse at one stage and he didn't say "no". He kind of said "yes" actually, but he said he'd have to buy some land from Ian Galvin first. Dad had his eye on the field next to our land that Ian owned, but Ian wouldn't part with his land so I never got my horse.

My cousin Anna and her cousin Jane spent a lot of time with us down in Garryvadden over the years. We'd have great times the four of us, that's Anna, Jane, Peter and myself. We'd go on trips to the beach, light bonfires, have barbeques, feed the horse down the lane, probably wade in the river, and if the weather was nice enough we'd have water fights.

That's something that I'd occasionally get to do with the children, or rather teenagers at this stage, on the road in Dublin. There's nothing like a good water fight on a lovely sunny day, but as sunny days are scarce in Dublin, or at least they were when I was growing up, these water fights were quite rare but I guess that's what made them so special and enjoyable.

I can recall two more seizures that I had in Dublin. I had so many seizures in my teen years, and my epilepsy was really eating me up, but some of the seizures stand out more than others. The first of these two seizures happened while I was on the way to school. I can remember cycling along the footpath on the side of the main road that our cul-de-sac was off, so I wasn't far from home when it happened. I had really just gone around the corner and up the path a little bit. Anyway, I was cycling my bike and I felt the seizure coming over me, so I got off my bike and let the seizure take hold of my body. When I came to, the woman who lived in the house I'd stopped in front of was standing beside me. I was able to give the woman my home number, so she phoned the house and got my dad. He hadn't gone to work yet. The woman told my dad the situation and said that she'd called an ambulance. Dad said to her,

"Don't call an ambulance".

Dad didn't want to have to go to the hospital to get me. The woman cancelled the ambulance and I suppose Dad came to pick me up and brought me home, but I have to say I don't remember that part at all. I'd probably have been kept out of school for some time after having the seizure, and there were probably more seizures on the way as well.

The other seizure happened outside as well, only this time it was in the evening. There was one night in my teen years when I was outside the house playing football with Alan from across the road. I fancied Alan at the time and I was really enjoying playing one-on-one football with him. Then all of a sudden I felt a seizure coming over me and I thought to myself, *'Oh no, I don't want Alan to see me having a seizure'*, so I quickly told him I was going and I started running down the side passage. Then Alan called out to me to tell me I'd forgotten my jacket so I had to go back to him. I was just coming up to the pillar when I collapsed onto the flowerbed. The next thing I knew, Dad was taking me into the house. During this time I kept looking back at Alan and Alan was looking at me. It was a good night with an unfortunate ending and I never really played football like that with Alan or with any man again.

By this time in my life I was more of a Wexford girl than a Dublin girl, and I had my eyes on the handsome Wexford men who I'd see as my Dad and myself were driving into Blackwater to get the paper, for example. I'd wave at them and they'd wave back, but I never really wanted to do more than talk to them, or any other man for that matter.

Now it was time for me to learn how to kiss and I wasn't sure how this was going to happen. Well, I'd been spending my Saturday nights in Seany O'Sheas pub in Blackwater, mainly sitting all on my own at the bar and after a while maybe making some contact with the teenagers in the pub. One time I asked the lads who were playing pool if I could play against one of them. I did, and not only did I play against him, but I beat him as well. He was really annoyed. Then one weekend I found out that there was a bus that went from Blackwater to Kilmuckridge bringing teenagers to a nightclub there. So, I started going to this nightclub. I can remember paying five pounds in and I think they took my coat but I'm not sure. I'd always have had my legs covered and was probably wearing jeans with a nice girlie top. I would have been wearing ankle boots as well. I never got into the expensive girlie habit of buying shoes and I'm still like that. I'm one of the few Dublin women who hate buying shoes. So, I was going to this nightclub all on my own but I got used to the routine pretty quickly.

I'd head into the club, which was basically just one big square room with a reasonable sized dance floor in the middle. There were seats and tables around three sides of the dance floor and the bar, which was basically the length of the dance floor or a bit longer, was on the fourth side. I'd always be the first on the dance floor and that's basically what I'd do all night. I'd dance and I'd drink pints of water throughout the night, which is a bit like what I do now in Dublin but I'd know a lot more people now and I'd mix more. Some of my favourite songs to dance to in this club were Abba songs, and I remember I particularly loved dancing to "Dancing queen". In fact I know that I was definitely going to this club at the age of seventeen, and in good shape, because I can still picture myself fitting right into the part of the song 'only seventeen'.

So I'd dance all night, then at the end of the night when the slow songs came on, I'd stand at the side of the dance floor and some man would always come over to ask me to dance. So I became an expert kisser, and actually a dangerously powerful kisser for a girl who wanted to keep her virginity. Although when I learned how to kiss it was all physical . . . there was no feeling, no emotion in it, because I never knew the person I was kissing.

One time when I was dancing on my own, a foreign man came over to me and started dancing with me. I didn't have a clue who this man was but I'll tell you something, he was a brilliant dancer. I was really enjoying dancing with him, he was dipping me and all. Then when the song was over he said to me,

"You're a very good dancer".

I replied,

"You're not bad yourself", but that was about the height of our conversation. I don't know if I even asked him what his name was.

There were three incidents involving men that happened to me in Wexford, and each one was worse than the previous one. The first one happened outside the club at the end of the night, when the man I'd had the slow dance with took me outside. I don't know his name because I hardly said a word to anybody in those days. I hardly know the names of any of the many men I danced with and kissed. Anyway, this man took me outside and put me up against the fence. He started kissing my neck and I could do nothing about it but just let him kiss away to his heart's content.

It felt a bit unpleasant, but I didn't really think anything of it. I'd never heard of love bites so I'd never have guessed he was biting me. Though I have to say he was very good at it, and I was actually quite enjoying it. It's all in the lips. When he stopped, I said I had to get my jacket so we went our separate ways. When I went to get my jacket the man who was giving it to me said,

"You've got some bad marks on your neck there".

I don't know why, but the reply I gave him was,

"Do you want a go?"

That shut him up, although I still didn't have any idea what my neck looked like.

Shortly after that, Mum came to collect me and brought me home. When I went into the house and Dad saw me he immediately said,

"WHO did that to you?"

His tone said, '*how dare anyone treat my precious daughter's body in that way*'. I just told him the complete truth.

"I don't know."

When I went into the bathroom I got an awful shock when I looked in the mirror and saw all the black circles all over my neck. I can't remember what it felt like going around in public with marks like those on my neck, but I'm sure it wasn't too bad, because if it was I would have remembered.

The second incident happened outside the club as well but it was way more uncomfortable. I was dancing with this particular man whose name I didn't know either. After the dance, for some reason I said to him,

"Do you want to go outside?"

That turned out to be a big mistake. Straight away he opened what seemed to me like fire escape doors and took me outside. When we got outside, we were in a kind of back yard area that was basically like a rubbish dump with lots of old metal machinery. I was very uncomfortable in this situation and I felt very vulnerable, so I said to the guy,

"I don't like it here at all. Can we go somewhere else?"

He seemed okay with this request so we headed over to the left-hand side, towards big gates made from sheets of metal. To the far side of the gates there was a pillar with soil or something beside it that we were able to climb up to. When we got up to the top of the pillar we looked down the other side, and it was a good distance down to the ground. We were really quite high up. Nevertheless, this guy managed to jump down on the other side. Then I played the poor little female role and jumped into his arms pretending to be a bit nervous. Now we were in an open area and I could see the road and the front of the club so I felt more comfortable, but I still wasn't in a good situation because this guy had only one thing on his mind, although I didn't know that yet.

He took my hand and he brought me up a little hill with trees on one side. He put me lying down on the grass beside the trees and basically had me pinned down on the ground. Next thing he opened my jeans and started fingering me. I said,

"Stop, stop, that hurts", but he didn't stop. I gave out a little scream and he said

"Shhh, Shhh".

He continued fingering me and said to me,

"You'll like it, it's very nice. It's very nice".

I just lay there and said nothing but in my mind there was no way I was going to lose my virginity. I didn't even know his name and making love on a hill didn't seem very special to me. Anyway, I lay there and let him finger away and kiss me, but then when he took his hands off me to open his jeans I was out of there. I stood up and grabbed my bra, which he'd taken off, but I still had my top on. It was a strapless bra and I remember that when he took it off he said,

"What's this?"

Then I walked away from him. As I was going I said to him,

"That wasn't very nice".

He said "SHIT!"

Mum was actually waiting in the car nearby so I got away from him quite promptly. When I got into the car I told her what had happened and asked her why he'd fingered me, because I actually thought it was pretty disgusting. Mum told me that men sometimes do that to excite a girl. Then she said to me,

"I wouldn't tell your Dad about this".

I said, "Why not?"

She said, "I just wouldn't".

So I kept it to myself.

The third incident happened at a different venue and a good few years afterwards, so I'll come back to it later in the book.

Sometimes in my teen years, between my studies and my epilepsy, there just didn't seem much point to life at all. I was nearly suicidal at times but anytime I was thinking that way I always knew that people loved me an awful lot. That's what kept me going through all the hard times. I have to say, the years up to and including third year and my Junior Cert weren't too bad. I actually won the 'Student of the year' award in third year in school. I can still remember Sr. Basil, the principal, outlining all the reasons why the particular student had won the award, before she announced who it was. One of the things that really stood out was when she said, "She always wears the proper uniform". When I heard her say that I thought straight away that's me, because hardly any of the girls in the school wore the proper uniform. Then she said my name and I had to walk up to the stage to get the award, which was basically a plaque with the school crest, and my name and junior cycle and 'Student of the year' written on it. I was delighted. Just before my Junior Cert, I got loads of good luck cards from neighbours and relations and maybe teachers in Mum's school as well. The sitting room was packed with cards. I did okay as well, and was quite happy with my results. I think I got four honours and five passes, which was pretty good for me.

As the years went on, life got harder and harder, and hoping became almost impossible. I remember one Christmas something that really touched my heart. It was a present that my grandmother gave me. Now as I mentioned earlier in the book, I rarely got anything I liked from my grandparents, but this year I was given something fabulous. I took my time taking the wrapping off as usual, and was hoping as hard I could but guessing that I wouldn't be excited by it. When I took the wrapping off, it was a picture frame with what looked like a poem inside it. I held it in front of me and started reading it. It was called '***Footprints***' and it went like this:

> *One night a man had a dream. He dreamed he was walking along the beach with the Lord. Across the sky flashed scenes from his life. For each scene he noticed two sets of footprints in the sand, one belonging to him the other to the Lord.*
>
> *When the last scene of his life flashed before him, he looked back at the footprints in the sand. He noticed that*

many times along the path of his life there was only one set of footprints. He also noticed that it happened at the very lowest and saddest times in his life.

This really bothered him and he questioned the Lord about it. "Lord, you said that once I decided to follow you, you'd walk with me all the way. But I have noticed that during the most troublesome times in my life, there is only one set of footprints. I don't understand why when I needed you most you would leave me."

The LORD replied, "My precious, precious child, I love you and I would never leave you. During your times of trial and suffering when you see only one set of footprints, it was then that I carried you.

When I came to the end of it a big smile came upon my face. I was thrilled with my Christmas present. I thanked my grandparents and I hung it up on my bedroom wall and it's still there to this very day.

After my Junior Cert I had to decide whether to do transition year or go straight into fifth year. I ended up going straight into fifth year, and I actually had to repeat the year. Maybe I would have been better doing transition year but that's just the way it happened. Life just seemed to be study, study, study and it was so hard. I was going through all this strain and hardship of education that wasn't really going anywhere. I was basically going through it all on my own as well. I still didn't really have any friends. I hung around with some of the neighbours in the evenings but I wouldn't have said very much.

My Uncle James, God rest his soul, one of my mother's brothers, died when I was in my teens, leaving behind him his wife and his five children. He'd been suffering from cancer for years and I can still remember the trips he made from Mayo to Dublin to see us and my grandparents, and he was probably getting treatment as well. The cancer started out as a lump on his back, but it was very close to the spine. The choice was to remove the lump and take the risk of losing the use of his legs, or to leave the lump there and go with other treatments. He took the option of other treatments but in the end they weren't good enough, and the cancer gradually spread through his body. I can remember looking at him in my grandparents' house and noticing that he didn't look too good, but I never dreamt that he was dying.

I think Uncle James's funeral was my third. My first was Mrs. Walsh in Wexford and my second was my mum's aunt, Kathleen, on my grandmother's side. She was a nun so she lived quite a good life. At her funeral, my mum's cousin, Fr. Richard said the mass, and they needed two people to bring up the gifts. Peter and myself were given this job to do, without any practice or guidance. When the time came, the two of us went over to the table with the gifts on it. Peter took the bread and I took the wine, but Peter went racing off ahead of me and I ended up dropping the cloth. When the cloth slipped off the chalice and onto the ground, I darted down really quickly to get it and then continued up the aisle. I was told afterwards that I didn't bow properly either, that I just nodded my head, so it was a bit of a disaster but Fr. Richard actually loved it. It was great preparation for Uncle James's funeral though. Peter and myself were given the job again, and it went very smoothly this time.

Chapter 24

So now I was preparing for my Leaving Cert, or at least trying to. I was so bad at all the subjects that I was going down to the pass level in every subject but one. The only subject I was still doing honours in was art, but I'd say you could have guessed that. Mum would be going through jobs that I might like to have or that I'd like to study for in college. I always wanted to be a teacher, I think a primary school teacher, but that was never going to happen because my Irish was pretty pathetic. I would have loved to be a vet but there was no way I'd have got the points for that, but it was nice to think about all the same.

My epilepsy was so bad in my teen years that they started considering me for surgery.

I had gone from doctor to doctor and I'd been put on different medications to try and control my epilepsy, but nothing was working. My brain had been photographed again but nothing showed up. According to the photos I had a perfect brain.

Anyway, I was brought into hospital and I was put in a room with another girl who was being considered for surgery. So I was in this room with wires attached to my head and I was being videoed, because they wanted to video me having a seizure. But the strange thing was that every time I went to the hospital, I'd never have a seizure. After about two weeks of waiting for me to have a seizure, they decided to take me off my medication to bring one on. Once they did that, I had loads of seizures and I was so bad that they had to give me medication through the rectum.

When I first heard about the idea of surgery to get rid of my epilepsy I jumped at the idea, but then I said to Dad,

"What's the worst that could happen?"

Dad replied, "You could die".

When I heard this I wasn't so keen on the idea, but in the end it turned out that I wouldn't have been able to have surgery anyway. What they would have done was remove the part of the brain that was damaged and in my case the temporal lobe, and let the other temporal lobe on the other side of the brain take over the memory. But even though the photos didn't pick up any damage to my brain the wires, which were attached to my head picked up activity on both sides while I was having the seizures so I wouldn't have been a candidate for surgery.

My epilepsy was really ruining my life, and at one stage in my teen years I started becoming psychotic after having seizures. I'd start thinking I was pregnant and that I was the mother of God, which was really disturbing and embarrassing, not only for myself but for family members too. I would have said other stuff as well that I don't want to go into, but I basically caused a lot of trouble that even involved the Gardai. Life was so bad during those years that there were times that I was down on my knees in my bedroom crying out to God in desperation to please take away my epilepsy. I was nearly begging him. I was saying the Our Father again and again. My epilepsy was really killing me.

I'd tend to have seizures at the most stressful times in my life and as my Leaving Cert exams got closer I became very stressed. As a result of this, I had a lot of seizures in the period just before it, which was a disaster. How was I supposed to sit my exams straight after having seizures? Because of my illness, I was able to sit my exams in a separate room with my own examiner. Once they were over, I was finished with secondary school, which was great. But when my results came three months later, I just took one look at them, then immediately handed the piece of paper to Mum and jumped face down onto the couch and burst out crying. After all that hard work and all that studying night after night with Mum, I didn't even get a Leaving Cert—I just got three passes. The worst result I got was in my first exam, the best result was in my last exam. That was the really frustrating thing . . . that you could see from the results getting better as my health improved, but at that stage it was too late.

There was one morning in my teen years when I don't know what came over me, but I decided to climb out my bedroom window onto the lower roof. I was sitting on the roof in my dressing gown feeling quite cold. Then I saw one of the neighbours across the road whose name was Ann, and I automatically waved at her with my arms to signal help!! She came across the road and called in next door to get another neighbour to watch me while she went to get a ladder. Ruth came out to me and as she was standing on the ground looking up at me she said,

"Go back up there and get back in that window".

I said to her, "I'm too cold to move".

A few minutes later Ann came back with a ladder and Ruth climbed up and helped me down to the ground. This incident gives a taste of the trouble I caused without even trying to, and it also shows what great neighbours we were, and still are, blessed with.

Now that I'd finished school I had to look for someone to come with me to my debs. Alan, one of the Logan boys who I'd had my eye on for years was the obvious first choice, but when I asked him he said "No". I was a bit taken aback by this so I said,

"Well, I have a lot of good-looking cousins I could bring".

All the same it didn't seem right to ask a cousin to take me to the debs so I decided to ask one of the other lads on the road. My second choice was Joe, so I went up to Joe's house and rang the doorbell. His mother answered the door and I said,

"Is Joe there?"

She said, "You mean Joseph".

I said "Sorry, Joseph".

She said he was out just then but asked if she could take a message.

I said "Well, I just wanted to see if he'd come to my debs with me".

She said, "I wish I could say yes. He'll be back in about an hour and you can ask him then".

I said "Okay" and I went home.

Later on I went to talk to Joe and he said that he was flattered to be asked but that he was a bit past that and he suggested Alan. I told him that I'd already asked Alan and he'd said "no". Joe said he'd talk to Alan for me. That night I went over to Alan's house and I talked to his dad. He told me that they had six men in their house and that one of them would come with me to my debs. So Alan ended up getting the job.

I had great fun picking out a dress with Mum. It was a straight, full length black velvet dress with bare shoulders and a stiff, shiny turquoise piece of material around the top. My godmother came over on the day of the debs with a big box of Milk Tray for me. Then Alan came over with my orchid and a smaller box of Milk Tray, and told me that he hadn't been able to get a waistcoat. For some reason I decided not to wear my orchid. I left it in the little jar with the intention of drawing it, which I did a day or two afterwards.

Mum brought Alan and myself up to the school. We went into the crowd and when I saw loads of couples holding hands I said to Alan,

"Hold my hand, hold my hand".

Alan said to me, "Link my arm".

So I linked my arm around Alan's arm and that was the beginning of the night. Still, I was really all on my own the same as usual. We hardly said a word to each other all night though I'm sure Alan had a great night. He did give me a dance though, so at least that was something. I remember going around complimenting the other men on their waistcoats. Some of the waistcoats were amazing and I remember playing cards on one of them.

I didn't really know anyone there. Well, obviously I knew some of the girls to see, but I didn't really know any of them well enough to talk to as we'd barely said a word to each other all through secondary school. I would have been too shy and self-conscious anyway. I remember going home with Alan the following morning. It was really cold and I said to him a few times,

"Give me your jacket, give me your jacket" but he wouldn't give it to me. All I could do was link my arm around his and lean into his body as hard as I could to try and keep myself warm. I can still remember racing into the house the next morning and I ran to my dad and told him how cold I was, but I warmed up quick enough. The debs was over and done with, but I wouldn't say it was a terribly enjoyable experience for me.

Chapter 25

After my Leaving Cert I did a post Leaving Cert course in Art and Design. Two elements of the course that I particularly enjoyed were weaving and stained glass. I was thrown in with quite a nice group of students and the college was near where my grandparents lived so I used to go up to their house at lunchtime. Sometimes I used to go outside to an area at the back of the college with one particular lad and we used to chat together while he smoked his cigarette, but I'd never have considered having a boyfriend who smoked, so that was out of the question. I actually think he quite liked me because towards the end of the year I remember him saying to me,

"Do you write?"

But we never kept in contact.

One evening a group of us went out to the back area and we started messing around, which wasn't like me at all. I had kind of unintentionally organised this game which was loosely based on the scene in '*Dirty Dancing*' where Johnny and Baby were on the tree trunk working on Baby's balancing skills. I was on this long narrow piece of metal, a bit like a narrow bar. The other girls in the group kept taking turns trying to get me off the bar but I kept knocking them off instead, so the object of the game was to see who could get me off the bar. It wasn't because I was very strong that I was knocking all the girls off, but I was keeping the secret of using my balance to myself, and none of the other girls thought about their balance. Eventually one of the lads noticed and said to the girl who was on the bar with me,

"Use your balance, use your balance". This particular girl knocked me straight off the bar and I went flying head first into the schoolbag of one of the other girls who was leaning up against a wall holding her bag in front of her. I was really shocked after this and I was thinking, oh my God if that girl hadn't been standing there I'd probably be dead.

It was during this year that I became very close to my grandmother. After all these years of having her around, I only started to build some kind of close relationship with her when I was about twenty, but little did I know that I didn't have much more time with her. Soon after that my grandma got stomach cancer, and since she was eighty eight years of age she decided not to fight it and to die at home in her own bed. I can still remember getting very upset when Mum told me that Grandma had cancer. I think I cried more for my grandma than for anyone or for anything else. I'm very strong emotionally, and I don't cry very much at all, at films or anything, but I definitely cried when I heard my grandma was dying.

I think my grandparents got someone to come in to help take care of my grandmother but I know that I helped to take care of her as well, because I still have a card that my grandma gave me. It's a card with a painting of the Rouen Cathedral in dull weather by Claude Monet with this message in my grandma's writing:

> *Dear Sarah,*
>
> *Thank you for all your help. Love always Grandma.*
>
> *Sunday 6th October '98*

My grandma died in January '99 and that was my fourth funeral. It was a beautiful funeral. I can still remember my grandma being carried up the aisle by her grandsons and one of her nephews. Grandma's other grandson was a fabulous boy soprano and he sang beautifully as she was being carried up the aisle. It really was very special. Peter and myself brought up the gifts, a job that we were becoming expert at doing.

After my grandmother died, my grandpa basically gave up the will to live. He was moved to a nursing home and he was there for a few months, but he died in August. They put pneumonia as the cause of death on his death cert, but I believe that if Grandma had been alive at the time he would have pulled through it. I can remember him saying to us on the day he died,

"I want to die".

He was ninety-two years of age.

The next big occasion was my twenty first birthday. There had to be some sort of a celebration for this birthday, and as I didn't have any friends and never went out drinking, we had a family barbeque in Garryvadden. We invited all the Dromeys and I'd say the Hurleys were invited as well. The Hurleys are my dad's step-siblings and their families. My twenty first birthday party is a bit of a blur really and as usual I'd say everybody else had a better time than I did, though I have to say it was my best birthday yet. On all my previous birthdays, I'd open presents as soon as I got them, rather than leaving them in a pile to open later. So I automatically did the same thing on my twenty first. I'd never got so many presents before in my life, so I spent a lot of time opening presents when I could have been playing with my cousins. There was one moment in particular during the party that I remember very clearly. It was when my Uncle Martin, my dad's second youngest brother, who happens to be my godfather as well, came into me in the kitchen with his daughter Anna, who was carrying a huge rectangular package. I opened it up and it was the most fabulous suitcase on wheels.

That was the focal point of my twenty first birthday party. The other thing I remember is that it took me ten breaths to blow out the twenty one candles. I think that was partly to do with my lungs. I could never really sense my left lung and I never really had control of it, which

I think was probably due to my epilepsy. Throughout my life, I was never able to blow out all my birthday candles in one go. Anyway, it took me ten breaths to blow out the twenty one candles and I can remember that the cake tasted gorgeous. It was a big chocolate cake that my mum had made using drinking chocolate. There was no kissing the birthday girl at my party, as the majority of guests were from the older generation. I didn't miss it though, as I'd never been at a party where the birthday girl, or boy for that matter, got a line of the opposite sex coming up to give you a birthday kiss. The first time I experienced that was at my cousin Anna's twenty first six years later.

A few weeks later, my aunt Michelle called with bad news. My uncle Hugh, one of my dad's older brothers, had died of a heart attack. Hugh and Michelle had three children, Jason, Adam and Sarah. They had lost their dad very early in their lives, and of course Michelle had lost her husband. I can still remember how upset they were at the removal. I particularly remember Jason, Sarah and Michelle with their arms around each other and in tears. I actually didn't know my uncle Hugh very well. We didn't have an awful lot of contact with them while I was growing up, as they lived quite a distance away and Jason and Adam are a good bit older than us.

Now my education had turned another corner and I was in Griffith College doing a six-month course called *Planning my Future*. One thing I loved about this course was that twice a week, we spent a section of the day in the gym, and I think I lost a lot of weight. I loved the gym and they also got us to do a communication workshop and learn first aid, and we got work experience as well. I really enjoyed the work experience which was in a graphic design company. I remember helping to design a logo for a company called *Inspiration* and my logo, which I think they used, was the image of a pencil where the I is in the word 'Inspiration', but once the time allotted for my work experience was over, I never went back there.

My social skills developed a bit while I was in Griffith College but, as usual, it was with lads. I was never very good at socialising with girls. All the same, once I'd finished the course the friendships faded away very quickly.

Chapter 26

Now my epilepsy was about to cause another disaster within the family. One evening I felt a seizure coming on me as I was going upstairs. When I felt it I got very scared so I ran down the stairs and in to my dad in the kitchen. Next thing I knew my dad and myself were flat out on my parents' bed. I spent the next week recovering from seizures and my dad was stuck in bed, physically unable to move. I had wrecked my dad's back.

At the time, we didn't know why my dad couldn't move, but he had a massive bruise on his back. Over time, my dad put two and two together and figured out what must have happened. When I came flying in to my dad as I was about to have the seizure, I pushed him very firmly back into the chair and Dad's braces must have dug very deep into his back, injuring him in the process.

My dad was never the same after that. He was able to walk again but not very well, and he'd always walk quite slowly. After that, the combination of his love for the freedom of alcohol and his walking disability wasn't good for his weight at all. I think I had set my dad on a downhill slope, but I never really thought about it that much as I was still trying to figure out my own life, which wasn't going very well, and I still had very bad epilepsy. My dad never blamed me for it either, and any time I did bring it up with him he always said that it wasn't my fault.

I missed my first wedding because of that seizure. My cousin Lisa, my mother's niece, was getting married to Alan who she'd been going out with for some time, and Dad and myself missed it. After that my cousin gave birth to my second first cousin once removed who they named Colette, and they've had three more since, another girl and two boys—perfectly balanced. My cousin Catherine, also on my mother's side of the family, had had a daughter previously in America who she named Niamh, then she had another daughter shortly after Colette was born, who she named Maeve.

Pretty soon after Lisa and Alan were married, I made it to my first wedding, the marriage of my cousin Jason, my dad's nephew, to Claire. Not long after that I had another first cousin once removed. Jason and Claire had a daughter who they named Gemma and they've had two more children since—a son, and another girl who was born at home in a sudden fifteen-minute labour. Everything worked out just fine thank God.

In terms of my education, it was the hospital that prompted the next turn in my life. They suggested that I go to a graphic design course for people with special needs in Parnell Square, opposite the Garden of Remembrance in the city centre. Well, I did have a flair for art so going in the direction of becoming a graphic designer wasn't a bad idea really. I started going to this course everyday for about five years. A lot happened while I was there. For starters, I was put on a medication to stop any psychotic activity which had a side effect of increasing your appetite. As a result of this, I put on loads of weight.

It was before I put on that weight that my third sexual incident happened in Garryvadden. I was in Seany O'Sheas pub in Blackwater village and this time I knew the man involved. While I was sitting in the pub I looked over to my right and I saw Ian Lynch, the grandson of the old woman up the hill, Mrs. Kelly. I had played with Ian and his sisters when we were younger. I had actually thought about him over the years and he'd obviously thought about me, because he came straight up to me and the two of us French kissed each other right there in the pub for everybody to see. Now, I still had no intention of losing my virginity but Ian had definitely not put it out of the question, but as usual we hardly talked at all. Since I was able to put some emotion into the kiss because I knew Ian, it aroused him straight away and he took my hand and brought me outside. It was dark, and there were a number of cars around us. He brought me over to the side beside some bushes and I don't know what he was doing with his hands but they were in his trousers. We didn't really make much eye contact but I must have given him the impression that I wasn't interested because he said to me,

"Will I put him away?"

I said "Yes!!" Then we went back into the pub.

Less than a minute after that Ian took me outside again. He brought me across the road and over the bridge and he opened the little gate to the small public garden beside the river. Now Ian definitely should have known, and probably did know, that I didn't want any of this but things got quite sexual in that garden. I'd say he was kissing my chest. I remember him sitting me on the bench and I think he wanted a blowjob. I just kept saying,

"Sorry, sorry".

And I didn't give him a blowjob. The most disturbing thing I remember about being in that garden, and I don't know if I'll ever forget it because it had quite an effect on me, was that all of a sudden he took my hand, placed it on his penis and told me to pull. What a horrible way to be introduced to that part of a man's body. You could say it was kind of scary. Anyway, I pulled it for him and that seemed to keep him happy.

The next thing I remember about that night was Ian offering me a ride home. I wasn't going to accept, but he persuaded me. His car was a three-door hatchback and Ian put me in the back seat, and there was another lad, whose name I wasn't told, sitting in the front seat. We drove off, and as the journey went on I just got more and more nervous. When Ian came to a junction in the road about a mile from my house he skidded in a circle, and that's when I realised he was planning on taking his friend home first and I was worried about what he had in mind for me. I was trapped in the back seat and was getting hysterical. I just kept saying to the other lad,

"Don't leave me in the car with him, don't leave me in the car with him".

In the end, the other lad got Ian to take me home. He just said to him,

"Ian, will you just take the girl home".

I was so relieved when Ian let me out of the car. I didn't look at him at all and I walked straight towards the gate into our house. Ian followed me and he said,

"Sarah, will you go out with me?"

The cheek of him. I briefly turned my head around and said "NO!!"

One Sunday after that when Mum, Dad and myself were driving up Garryvadden hill on our way back to Dublin, Ian was at his uncle's gate with his uncle and another man. I actually didn't notice, but Mum said to me after we'd passed them,

"Ian blushed".

I didn't say anything to anyone, I just kept it to myself.

Chapter 27

The course that the hospital suggested I should attend was run by an organisation called the Irish Social Firms Initiative (ISFI). When I started off there I was quite shy and I was still very sick with epilepsy, but no one got annoyed in any way if you needed to take time off from the course for your health. Everything was much the same when you got back and you worked at your own pace.

Design Forum was the name of the company that was running the graphic design course for people with special needs. There were art classes and classes for different software packages on the computers like Quark Xpress and Photoshop. There were other courses within ISFI as well for people with special needs that were similar to Design Forum. I think there was a restaurant and I know there was definitely a secretarial section as well.

There was a mixture of men and women and everyone who was there was in the same boat. We all had one thing or another that had happened to us to affect our health. We all stuck together and if any of us were in hospital we'd make a card for the person and everyone would sign it. When I went there first, one of the girls whose name was Jenny persuaded me to do the women's mini-marathon. I took part but my health wasn't good enough and my body wasn't strong enough, and I had a seizure and ended up in hospital.

Gerry, one of the other members of the group, made a card for me and everyone signed it. It was on an A3 sheet of paper with a really nice image of a beautiful lady in a pretty purple dress with lovely long, flowing golden hair. It had 'Get well Sarah' printed beneath the picture and Gerry had written his message and signed it underneath. And he'd got everyone else in the course to sign it as well. So, I had a lovely laminated sheet of A3 paper with lots of new friends who had signed it for me. I was thrilled, and I hung it up in my bedroom and I had it there for quite a few years.

The course was doing wonders for my social skills. Gerry was the first person to take me under his wing and, as usual, I mixed better with the men than with the women. As time went on I latched on to different men. Peter McFadden was the first man that I took a shine to. Peter and myself used to spend time in the art room doing crosswords together. Now Peter smoked, but I took such a shine to him that the smoking didn't bother me that much. I gradually started putting on more and more weight because the medication I was on gave me a huge appetite. I was eating really big portions and I remember going to Eddie Rockets at lunchtime in town and I was eating lots of fatty foods there, so I was bound to be putting on weight.

The doctors were trying me with different medications to control my epilepsy but they weren't working. I was still having seizures. I was going from doctor to doctor as well. I was on a waiting list for a Dr. Delanty who was supposed to be very good and had trained in America so we, that's myself and my parents, were waiting to see how that would go.

I wouldn't have been socialising much outside the course, but Peter and myself used to walk down O'Connell street at the end of the day together. We'd hug each other before we parted to go our separate ways so I guess we had some sort of relationship going. I was putting on a lot of weight though so I wouldn't have been very pleasing to the eye. One night, I think it was probably some sort of social occasion with the course, Peter saw me to a taxi and gave me a hug before we parted. When I got into the taxi the driver called Peter my boyfriend and I had to tell him that Peter wasn't my boyfriend. After that I decided that I had to find out where my relationship with Peter was going. The next day at lunchtime in ISFI,

I asked Peter if he'd walk down to the shop with me. He did, and while we were walking I mentioned the word boyfriend and that frightened him away big time, so that was the end of that. It didn't really bother me that much at all and things weren't too awkward on the course, maybe just a little bit.

During my time in ISFI, a new member of staff came along. Her name was Una and she was from Co. Sligo. Una really took a shine to me and we spent quite some time chatting together in the canteen. She was lovely and she helped me a lot throughout my years there. There was one stage when I kept saying to Una,

"I'm not normal" and she kept saying,

"You are normal", over and over again, and eventually I gave in. That's why when I hear people saying the word "normal" to describe someone instead of "healthy", it gets on my nerves.

Eventually I became a patient of Dr. Delanty and I remember really taking to him and admiring the way he was treating me. After meeting him the first few times I rarely saw him after that. This was because I was going public every three months or so and waiting at least an hour to be seen, usually by some foreign doctor who said the same thing every time. The one thing I always remember being asked was,

"Do you take a drink?"

So my epilepsy still wasn't getting any better.

In 2003, a new member joined us at ISFI. His name was Michael Cullen and he was from Cork. Michael was small enough in height and he had dark spiked hair. Michael really took to me the very first day, which wasn't that good because he suffered from anorexia and as I was going to Unislim, I wasn't eating much myself. I remember losing seven pounds the week Michael came to ISFI. We went to HMV together but I don't think he bought me anything. Then he decided we'd go to the cinema together. Now at this particular time in my life I didn't go to the cinema that often whereas I go all the time now. I didn't even know the names of most of the actors, though I would have watched loads of films at home.

The first Pirates of the Caribbean film had just come out in the cinema in Dublin but Michael wanted to go to a film that had Billy Connolly acting in it—I don't remember the name of the film. I didn't want to see Billy Connolly but I wanted to see Pirates of the Caribbean, so I said, "We'll flip a coin". We flipped a coin and I won so we ended up going to Pirates of the Caribbean. Neither Michael nor myself enjoyed the film that day but now it's my favourite film. It's very hard to choose a favourite film these days but I've come to realise that it's 'Pirates of the Caribbean: The Curse of the Black Pearl', at the moment anyway. I've yet to see "On Stranger Tides". The thing is I've absolutely fallen for Captain Jack. I love him so much and it's through Captain Jack that I've come to love Johnny Depp, but that's a totally different story and I'll probably touch on it later in the book.

Then Michael took me to a pub and I'm sure he bought me a drink. He started telling me things he'd been through in the past . . . things that he shouldn't really have been telling me as they were quite deep and I didn't know him very long. Sometime not long after that, he took me for a game of pool not far from where he was living. As I love pool I said to him, 'the best of three'. We started playing and we won a frame each. The best thing a lady can do while playing against a man is not to tell him you're any good. You've a way better chance of beating him that way. Anyway, we were on the third and final frame and Michael was really getting worried. I'll never forget the way he said "Sweet Jesus" when I potted a ball or he just missed or such like. It actually came down to a black ball game and match. In the end I potted the black in the wrong pocket so he won.

After that, we were in a café one day in town and I said, without thinking,

"I love talking to you".

Michael said, "Oh, come on" and he got up and started walking away from me. He hardly looked at me after that which quite upset me because I was really enjoying his company. You see, Michael was giving me all the wrong signals. I didn't know whether he wanted me or not. It really was quite a messy relationship that was kind of just floating along. In the end, I felt that Michael wasn't very nice to me so things were a little bit uncomfortable in Design Forum after that, but nothing I couldn't handle.

At some stage while I was on the course there was a social occasion of some sort where the different sections got together. It was at this time that I met Clare, who is now my best friend. We made eye contact and we recognised each other. Clare and myself had gone to the same primary school together but had never talked. Clare is an identical twin, and you know how twins stand out in a crowd. I recognised her as one of the twins with the two pigtails. I'm sure Clare recognised me as the miserable little girl who used to walk around the schoolyard all on her own. Anyway, we approached each other and got to know each other and we're still very good friends and we keep in contact with each other. Sometime after this I felt love outside the home for the first time. Clare was leaving our house after visiting me and she gave me a hug. I felt love in my heart, like something I'd never felt before.

Chapter 28

It was around this time that I got invited to my second wedding. My cousin Rachel was getting married to Joe. For this wedding I was far more sure of myself and much more confident as I had lost loads of weight, so I had a great time altogether. I loved the way the church was decorated with a flower on the side of each row of seats all the way up the aisle. I thought my cousin's dress was gorgeous and the pretty little flower girl wore a lovely white dress. The bridesmaids were beautiful as well, wearing wine full length, plain but very elegant dresses.

I had great fun mingling at the reception with all of Rachel's male cousins on the other side of the family. I was going around chatting to everyone, full of confidence. When I got back to ISFI, I started chatting to all the men, one after the other. It was my introduction to being a real flirt.

Shortly after that I went to Sicily with my parents and the first night we were there Mount Etna erupted at three o'clock in the morning. I didn't feel a thing, and I wouldn't have known at all if I hadn't been told. It did make our holiday more exciting though. One of the days we were there we took a bus journey up the mountain. They couldn't take us all the way up, but they took us up a good way and then let us out to wander around a bit. I collected a little bit of magma to bring home and I still have it to this day. While we were standing near the bus there was an aftershock and the ground shook. I thought it was great—an unusual, out of the ordinary experience.

While I was in Sicily I really enjoyed going around the shops and seeing a lot of Pinocchio puppets in nearly every shop we went into. It was the same puppet in lots of different sizes. We stayed in a lovely hotel, and the name of our waiter in the dining room was Casablanca, which I obviously never had any problem remembering. I remember my dad saying to him,

"Your mother loved the film so much that she named you after it".

It was lovely staying in a hotel and having our own waiter. It really was a great holiday.

After a week in Sicily it was back to Dublin and into ISFI again. I got straight back to flirting with a good handful of men who were on the course as well. They were all training to be graphic designers. I was doing mostly graphic design work as well, learning the packages which at that stage would have been mostly Photoshop. I have to say though, that course actually benefited me a lot socially rather than for the actual direction I wanted to take in life. I'd never dreamt of being a graphic designer, and I hadn't chosen the course myself but I really enjoyed it and gained a lot from it.

One evening I was at home in Dublin relaxing in the sitting room when my dad came into me. Then totally out of the blue he said to me,

"Sarah, would you like a dog?"

I jumped at the idea and immediately said "Yes".

I didn't realise it at the time, but Dad was actually using me in order for him to get a dog. All the same, I was thrilled with the idea of having a dog as I'd always wanted one in the past. Mum would never have wanted one and Peter wouldn't have been thrilled with the idea either.

Once I realised there was a chance that I could have a dog, I immediately started persuading Mum and Peter to agree to get one. After quite a bit of arguing at the kitchen table, Mum finally gave in and Dad was given permission to start looking for a dog. Of course I got the title of owner so I had some responsibility on my shoulders already. The great thing about being the owner was that I got to choose what kind of dog we were going to get.

Mum said she loved Labradors because they have a lovely face, but I had the idea of a retriever on my mind. So Dad found a mixed breed of Labrador/Retriever in 'Buy and Sell' magazine. I also said I'd like a female and the colour I had in mind was golden. It was a woman in Co Carlow who had four female puppies, three were white and one of them was golden. I can still remember being handed that beautiful little golden puppy into my arms. She was adorable. Dad said to me,

"Now Sarah, there's your dog".

The lady told us when she was giving us the dog that the two of us, the puppy and myself, would be nervous at first. We were too. I remember her shaking and me feeling a bit anxious as well. Everything eased though when I saw my dog's little golden tail start wagging. She was sitting on my lap and I was happy to be constantly petting my new little puppy as we were travelling back up to Dublin in the car.

Next it was time to pick a name for our new dog. We had a discussion about it and in the end we all agreed on the name Sandy, like in the film Annie, which I used to watch constantly as a child. Mum was great the way she took on the task of cleaning up Sandy's dirt when she was being toilet trained. Mum took a lot of the responsibility and after a while, even though I had come to realise the disadvantages of having a dog, we still had a beautiful, friendly and gentle dog and the weight wasn't all on me. Actually it was hardly on me at all. I just had to put up with the dog hairs, clean up after her on walks, help to bath her and maybe sometimes give her water or food, which wasn't that much at all.

I was still trying to lose weight and was going to Unislim, which was really working for me. The two things we were advised to do were walking, and drinking lots of water. We were told that these were the two main things that would help you to lose weight, and as Sandy needed to be taken for walks she was a big incentive to get outside and walk. I wouldn't have taken Sandy out walking every day. Mum would have taken her out as well.

When I got home after being in ISFI for the day, I'd stand in the kitchen with my back to the wall and I'd watch and wait while Dad cooked the dinner. Dad had become a great cook, which really just came from practice and from some advice from Mum, who was a great cook and baker as I've mentioned previously. When Dad retired due to injury, Mum decided that she'd cooked enough dinners and she handed the burden on to Dad.

One day I was in the kitchen with Dad and he told me about something he'd read in the paper. Dad would spend a lot of time going through The Irish Times every day and this particular day he'd found something very interesting. He'd seen an ad in the paper for a spiritual healer called Mary Malone. My epilepsy was still holding me back in life, and although things weren't as bad as they'd been in secondary school, they were bad enough. I'd almost given up on the idea that things might get better for me, but this gave me a bit of hope.

Now I'd gone to a healer already, who claimed that he had some power in his hands. I remember lying on a bench in my t-shirt while he kind of hovered his hands over my body. He hadn't done me any good, but now there was another chance. So Dad and myself started planning our trip down to Cork where Mary Malone was based at the time. I can remember wandering around Cork before it was time to go to see her. Dad and myself were passing a jeweller's shop, and I looked in the window and saw this gorgeous claddagh ring. It was gold and it had diamonds around the outside of the heart and an emerald in the centre of the heart. Next thing, very unexpectedly, Dad said to me,

"Do you want it?"

I couldn't believe it. I'd never expected him to buy it for me but I guess I just nodded my head and said "Yes". I was delighted.

When we met Mary Malone she brought the two of us into a room with her. I can't picture the room very well but I do remember her sitting me down on a chair. I can also picture very clearly the way she rotated her hand around my head. She had rosary beads in her hand and I can still remember the sensation as the rosary beads gently rolled around on my head. It felt lovely. I think she was praying as well as she moved her hand around. When she was finished, she gave me some sheets of paper with the same prayer on each sheet and she told me to give them to at least two people.

As the majority of my friends were the men in ISFI I gave the prayer to two of them—James O'Connor and Michael Cullen. I gave one to Michael as I was always interested in any way of communicating with him, as things had got quite awkward and he'd become very closed off since I told him that I loved talking to him. He took the prayer from me in the end but didn't really say much to me at all. I gave the other prayer to James as I knew there was definitely a religious side to him. I certainly didn't picture him as being a big part of my life in the future. James had long hair and a beard and lots of freckles, things that I definitely wouldn't have wanted in a man. His hair was kind of sandy coloured and you'd know that he carried a red gene and redheads really aren't my preference. James definitely had a religious side to him though, unlike all the other men.

At this stage, I'd been going to ISFI for about four years and the list of FETAC subjects I had to qualify in was getting shorter and shorter. There were only about two or three left for me to do. The two I remember were Maths and Work Experience. Work Experience was very difficult to get, and the issue of Maths brought the Leaving Cert back into the equation. I'd failed my Leaving Cert because I only passed three subjects, but if I could pass two more subjects I would have a Leaving Cert. It would be a pathetic Leaving Cert, but at least I'd have one. Now none of this was my idea, it all came from Mum and Dad and when I first heard it mentioned, I wasn't happy at all. After a lot of persuading, I finally agreed with Mum and Dad that I'd repeat the Leaving Cert. The other subject we decided I'd do was foundation Irish. Dad did some work on Irish with me but I was pretty confident that I could pass foundation Irish without doing too much homework.

So, I got started working on my Maths with a lot of help from Mum. I'd bring my Maths book with me into ISFI and I'd work on it at the big table in the art room. I worked very hard on my Maths and then when the time came to do my exams I got the privilege of having my own room and my own supervisor once again. When I got my results I was very satisfied with what I got. I got a D1 in maths and a B2 in foundation Irish. Now I had a leaving cert, and I was very happy.

The only thing that was left was Work Experience and my dad helped me to try to get some kind of work in graphic design. I was still going into ISFI for the social side, and my social skills just kept growing all the time, which was great. Dad and myself started going through the Yellow Pages under the heading of graphic design. There was a huge list of different graphic design companies all over Dublin. We went through them and picked out all the ones that were accessible for me. Then we typed up a letter explaining the situation to the manager of each company, asking them if they'd be able to give me some work experience. I'd say we sent out at least twenty letters to different companies. I got a reply from a neighbour who lives across the road and I hadn't even realised that he was one of the people I'd posted my letter to. Anyway, he said he'd commission me to do some work for him which I did.

I got one other reply from a company called Nameplate. I did some work experience with them and I quite enjoyed it, but I didn't really look for any opportunity to stay on with them. You see, deep down I didn't really want a job. I was progressing and having a lot of fun where I was. I loved ISFI and all of my friends there. The man in Nameplate filled out the form I needed completed in order for me to get a FETAC qualification in Work Experience. Now that module was done and dusted as well, but as I said above, I kept going in to ISFI to work on the computers and socialise with my friends, which I loved.

When I'd finished all the modules, I'd bring in illustrations of film characters like Shrek, for example. I'd scan them into the computer and trace them in Illustrator, a computer package, which I came to love working on. When I had the character traced, I'd print it out and show it to my friends to see what they thought. They'd give their opinion and I would then go back to the computer and I might work on it a bit more until I got a 'good', or you could say a 'perfect' verdict from my friends.

On one of our social outings, a large group of us went to climb Bray Head, which was quite steep. I remember climbing up the hill through the trees with only Michael ahead of me. I'd been chasing Michael for quite some time now. I still didn't really know what to make of my relationship with him. Anyway, Michael was the only person ahead of me and at one stage I said to him,

"Am I holding you back?"

Michael turned around and held out his hand for me to take. I took his hand and he helped me up the hill a bit but that was about all that went on between us that day, which was actually more than usual. Michael was still closed off from me and didn't want any type of communication at all. This was all because I'd said to him,

"I love talking to you".

After a good number of us had reached the top, we just turned around and started heading down again. Not long after I'd started going back down I slipped and landed flat on my bum. Jim, another man in the group, helped me up and then he continued to hold my hand and helped me down all the way to the bottom.

When we got back to the town, Jim and myself went into an arcade and played a game of pool. I won, but I didn't tell anyone afterwards. I think Jim had his eye on me all the time after that but I was never interested in him. I guess I was still trying to fix things between Michael and myself. My relationship with Peter had to be sorted out as well of course, in my book anyway. I didn't like the way we were ignoring each other.

Chapter 29

It was actually while I was studying my Maths that I decided it was time to fix things with Peter. I put my Maths workbooks into my bag and when I was leaving the art room where Peter and a couple of the others were situated, I said goodbye to everyone. Then I said to Peter,

"See ya Peter".

Then I told him to look at me. After quite a bit of persuasion, Peter finally lifted his head and said in a lower voice,

"See ya".

After that day things were great between Peter and myself, and I think he actually had his eye on me from then on. You see I'd lost all the weight that I was carrying when I suggested boyfriend/girlfriend and I was a lot easier on the eye. He never got me all the same as I was starting to fall for the last person I would have chosen to be my boyfriend, James.

I didn't have a party for my twenty-fifth birthday, which was nothing new, but I was given a lovely birthday card from Edward that he'd got everyone to sign. I'd been spending quite some time in the canteen with Edward and another young lad whose name was George. George was quite simple and quite a gas character, but God love him he even had a problem controlling his saliva. Anyway, Edward had got this card for me, and one of the women in the group had put 'quarter century woman' on it. When my Dad, God rest his soul, saw that he thought it was gas. James had signed it too, but I could hardly make out his writing. After talking to one of the other women on the course I made out what he'd written.

> *To Sarah, Happy Birthday Don't forget your shovel 50p Jamie.*

It summed up James perfectly and I actually thought it was kind of sweet, although there was still a long way to go before I'd even consider him as a friend. He was still just one of the group, but I have to say that he stood out because he really was quite an odd character.

It was around this time that I made the best decision I ever made in my life. I said to my dad one evening that I thought I wasn't getting anywhere with my epilepsy by going public, because even though I was under Dr. Delanty, I hardly saw him at all. The doctors I was seeing weren't doing me any good. I suggested that it would be better if I went to see Dr. Delanty privately, so we started doing that. I hadn't been going private long at all when he put me on a new medication called Keppra. This new medication, along with another medication called Lamictal, saved my life or you could maybe say that it gave me a new outlook on my life. I started to grow to become a new person and this happened around the same time that James started coming into my life.

The first impression I had of James, who was known to everybody as Jamie, wasn't very good at all. I thought he was a bit mad. He had this saying which he used to say to everybody so many times a day, "Don't forget your shovel", which he got from Christy Moore. He was mad about Christy Moore but I didn't know this at the time. He used to come out with "fifty pence" when he was leaving. He'd be telling pretty bad jokes throughout the day as well. He'd start laughing for no particular reason too, which I thought was really weird. I started to describe him as the guy who laughs at his own jokes. It's quite unbelievable that he actually became my boyfriend, but I'm pretty sure that the religious side of him had a big part to play in that.

I remember the first time I hugged James. Another member of our group, Shelly was walking ahead of me towards the back room. James was at the door and Shelly gave him a big hug. When I saw Shelly giving James a hug I decided to do the same, so I gave James a big hug. I think he was quite taken aback, but he just continued on with whatever he was doing beforehand.

After that, we started to become friends. We'd talk in the canteen upstairs for ages. I don't know what in God's name we'd be talking about, maybe religion. Maybe I was telling him all about my epilepsy, and how long I'd been fighting it. Anyway we'd talk and talk. One day we were up in the canteen talking to each other for three hours and we didn't realise it. Though I have to say James was the kind of person who couldn't stop talking.

One day when we were up in the canteen James told me that his sister was getting married and that he was going to be singing at the wedding. That was the one big thing James had going for him. He could sing, and he had a fabulous voice and even better he had fabulous tone. Some people can sing but James, he had fabulous tone. When he told me he'd be singing at the wedding I asked him if he was nervous, and he said he was a little bit but he didn't say much else.

Soon after that, I asked James if he had an e-mail address and he gave it to me. Then we started messaging each other and that's when I started to realise how bad his English was. James started this habit of sending postcards to each other from the allposters website. We'd pick out posters and write a message beside it and send it to each other. Since there was so much feeling in the poster alone the fact that James's English was so bad didn't really stand out very much.

On the last sports day that took place in ISFI, James brought his guitar. I was delighted because his guitar and his voice were his strong points. He ended up not playing his guitar at all and not singing either. What did happen though, was that I played football with the ISFI team. As you'll know from earlier, I love football so after persuading the manager of ISFI that I was healthy enough to play, I kind of captained our team. We kept winning game after game and we made it to the final. We didn't win the final as there was a very good female player on the opposite team who basically won it for them. We all got a silver medal for coming second though, which was nice.

Back in Garryvadden, Dad was planning to knock down the old house and build a new and better house instead. Up in Dublin I was falling for James but I didn't realise it at all. I still thought I was just spending time with him as one of the group and we were nothing more than friends. There was one day when we walked down O'Connell Street together and just before we went to cross O'Connell Bridge James loosely suggested that I might come over to his house sometime. I got a bit of a shock when I heard this, as I didn't want to go over to his house at all. All the same I was very nice about it and said something like,

"Okay James, thanks".

There was also one of the messages that he sent me where he left his home phone number. I still didn't view our relationship as being anything more than friends.

A few weeks later, I decided that I'd go down to Garryvadden with my dad for a little holiday and I also wanted to see any progress with the new house. I wasn't going down to Garryvadden that much anymore as my epilepsy was well under control, I was more independent and I was allowed to stay in Dublin on my own. So I went down with Dad for about a week. I really enjoyed watching Ian and Dad working on the foundations of the new house, which they were building just behind the old one. Then when I got back to Dublin, something inside me, for some reason, was feeling that I really would like to be talking to James. So I went and got his phone number from the computer and I decided to phone him.

James's father answered the phone with a very strong Dublin accent. I said to him,

"Can I speak to James?"

Then I could hear his father shout out "James", and after a few minutes James came on the phone. I told him who I was and then I suggested that we meet up on Saturday in Liffey Valley shopping centre, because James lived quite near there. I don't remember much about this meeting with James, but there are two things that stand out very clearly. The first thing is meeting a very unusual looking couple that James knew. The woman had very long, pure black hair with a full fringe and she was covered in make-up. She was with a man smaller than her, who looked foreign and hardly said a word. She did all the talking and I remember her saying to James,

"Is this the new girlfriend?"

James said, "Well, we're just friends".

She said, "That's the way it starts".

It was because of her that James and myself became a couple, because when she said the word girlfriend I liked the sound of it and I thought to myself, girlfriend. I could be someone's girlfriend. The other thing I remember about that day was James buying me a Van Morrison disc. I didn't know it, but this was the start of James buying gift after gift after gift for me. In the end, he was trying to buy my love but that's one thing about me, I'm not to be bought.

Chapter 30

I had now decided that I was James's girlfriend but I definitely hadn't considered anything more than that. I guess I just liked the idea more than anything, but I must have felt something for him because after a while our relationship did progress into being more than just friends. The following week I sat beside James pretty well all the time and I did these games with him that he was working on. They were similar to word searches and I couldn't believe how bad he was at them. Anyway, I was helping him and we were working, or you could say playing away with them, and I was probably laughing or at least giggling.

That's one thing I did a lot with James . . . laugh. I laughed more than I ever had in my life. A huge part of my relationship with James was laughing but I have to say that I was probably laughing *at* him more of the time than *with* him. We rarely laughed at something together but I was laughing at him more and more as the relationship went on and I loved it. I loved laughing at him but I didn't really love him as a person, just as a friend, but I never told him that. You see I don't think James had much respect for himself so it didn't bother him if I was getting great pleasure out of laughing at him.

The following Friday evening James and myself left ISFI together and as we were leaving I asked him to carry my portfolio for me, which he did. We crossed O'Connell Bridge and then just before we went our separate ways I said to him,

"Do you want to see me again on Saturday?"

James said "Yes", so we decided we'd meet in Bewleys Café, which was still on Westmoreland Street at the time. Then he gave me my portfolio and we parted for the evening.

On the Saturday at the end of October, James took me to the National Gallery of Ireland on Merrion Square in Dublin. Another way James got me to laugh was to make fun of someone else like poor George from ISFI, for instance. George was really a child and he couldn't look at a naked body for some reason. When we were in this art gallery, James started to bring up George when we were looking at the beautiful works of art of naked women. James would make me laugh by mentioning George and it worked. I really enjoyed myself. It was that evening that James bought me a diary, two calendars and a magnet of one of Monet's beautiful paintings.

I eventually managed to get James's arm around me. I had to keep kind of pushing into him to try and get him to put his arm around me and he did in the end. Then he asked me if it was okay. I said, "Of course". Then when we were sitting down on a bench in the gallery James told me to close my eyes. So I closed my eyes a bit nervously and he put a little heart in my hand and told me to open my eyes. He also said,

"It's not what you think".

I didn't know what he was going on about but what I was looking at was a felt heart in the form of a box you'd give someone a ring in. I nervously lifted the top of the heart and inside was a little silver crib with Mary, Joseph, baby Jesus, the donkey and a cow. I said to James,

"You shouldn't have".

Then I put it away and we went on looking at more of the beautiful works of artists from all over the world.

Afterwards we went into a pub for a drink and then James walked me to the bus stop. While we were waiting for the bus I asked him to sing to me, and he sang Van Morrison's "Have I Told You Lately" to me. I don't know if he learned it especially for me or what, but that was the song that he ended up singing to me an awful lot throughout our whole relationship. It's funny, when James sang songs to me I would never have related much to the words. What I would have been thinking was how well he was singing it and what other people who heard it would be thinking.

Back in ISFI again on Monday, people were beginning to see that James and myself were now a couple. I have to say I was really enjoying being his girlfriend and I'm sure he was really enjoying having me as his girlfriend. Obviously I never realised that I didn't actually love him as a person, but the thing was I didn't dislike him either and the two of us were enjoying some harmless fun that was new for both of us. Later that day, the two of us were talking in the canteen at some stage, and Jim was up there as well. Jim was the guy who helped me down the steep slope in Bray and played pool with me. When Jim saw the way that James and myself were talking he said to James,

"Are you stealing my girl?"

James replied, "Don't tell anyone".

This was something James used to say if he was ever in a sticky situation. I was thinking to myself, *'yea, he is, what are you going to do about it'*, but I didn't say anything.

One day James and myself were standing in the art room with our arms around each other. One of the members, Donal came into the room. He said to us,

"Will the two of you get a room?"

Then he said,

"You had a room until I came into it", which I thought was quite funny.

After the day was over in ISFI James and myself would go to a café or a pub and we'd talk and talk. That was the thing with the two of us—we were able to tell each other things that we'd tell nobody else. We understood each other and related to each other in the way that we'd both gone through hard times in the past, and we kind of consoled each other by talking about it.

James and myself had been boyfriend/girlfriend for about a week now and we hadn't kissed. The first time he kissed me was after our first trip to the cinema together to see *'Bridget Jones: The Edge of Reason'*. We didn't particularly enjoy the film and as we were leaving our seats James gave me a kiss on the cheek. I didn't do anything. I just kept making my way out of the cinema and James followed me. As the time went on I was beginning to realise that James had never French kissed a girl in his whole life and he was twenty-nine.

One day James and myself were at a pedestrian crossing and we were kissing while we were waiting for the green man. All of sudden a voice came from behind us "EXCUSE ME". It was George from ISFI and he obviously didn't like the way we were kissing in public. We stopped kissing and said, "Hello George". We got quite a laugh out of that.

James kept walking into lampposts and he used to make a joke out of it, which in one way I found funny and in another way I found embarrassing. Another thing I found extremely embarrassing was James using the public phones to phone his mother to tell her what he was doing. I mean we were in the twentieth century and I was surprised that James didn't have a mobile phone, and the fact that he was phoning his mother all the time was quite annoying.

Chapter 31

I remember the first time I went to James's house and met his parents. James and myself were in O'Briens café in the Ilac shopping centre and I suggested that I go back to his house with him. James said he'd phone his mother. You see James had to get permission from his mother to do anything, or at least close enough to anything. He was such a Mammy's boy. His mother did everything for him. She even bought his clothes for him. Anyway, James's mum said I could go back to their house so I did. I met his parents and found out that I was to call his mother "Mary" and his father "Fred", so that was that sorted, and I can remember Mary getting James to check his room before he invited me up to it.

Something I remember very clearly from my first visit was discovering that James had no manners. He offered me a hazelnut yogurt and he had one himself. I'm sure that when Mary, James's mother saw me eating she said out loud, "He has no manners". I would have thought to myself, "And whose fault is that? It's not his fault anyway". The thing that disgusted me the most was when James licked the yogurt lid right in front of me. It was disgusting, but as I think back on it now I have a laugh and think well, at least he could do something with his tongue.

One evening when we were up in James's bedroom I decided to say to him,

"Have you ever really kissed a girl?"

He must have said "No ", because it was quite obvious that he hadn't anyway. So, I had to teach him how to French kiss a girl and I didn't do a good job of it because throughout our five year relationship I never really enjoyed kissing him that much. He couldn't kiss at all and it's actually amazing that the relationship lasted, but I'd say it was because he loved me so much.

We spent our first Valentine's Day apart because my parents had booked a holiday for a week in Lanzarote and I was going with them. I was quite disappointed that I was going to be so far away from James for our first Valentine's Day. My Aunt Rose and Uncle Jack were with us in Lanzarote. Jack wasn't looking very well at all but they both seemed to be in fairly good form. The weather wasn't great at all and I think it was actually quite wet. The weather had never been that great anytime we went to Lanzarote which was probably because of the time of the year. My parents always went in February.

Even in the wet weather I'd walk down at least once a day to the place where you could go on the internet and I'd write a love letter to James and tell him what I was doing, what the weather was like etc., and I'd always tell him how much I missed him. After all I was stuck here in this miserable weather with my parents and nothing to do. The thing I enjoyed the most was when the five of us Mum, Dad, Rose, Jack and myself went out for dinner every evening and for dessert I'd always order a banana split. I had great fun comparing the banana splits in the different restaurants and deciding which one was the best.

I bought James a mobile phone for his birthday and he was delighted. Now, the embarrassment of James using payphones was dealt with. Early on in our relationship I can remember kissing James and then pulling away and saying "Oh, my lips". I had very sensitive lips and James had a beard but he loved me so much that he shaved off his beard. I'd say another reason he did it was so he wouldn't have to put up with me saying "Oh, my lips" anytime he went to kiss me as well.

Early on in our relationship James asked me to go to Roscommon with him and I said I would. As James didn't drive, his friend Darren drove the three of us down, and we stayed with their friend Alex and his wife Aisling, who obviously wanted to meet me. James had brought his guitar with him and I was delighted about that. I think the fact that I was getting so much attention from James's friends and everyone wanting me to tell them how James and myself started going out got on Aisling's nerves. Later on in the evening, when James was singing and playing his guitar someone asked him to sing Paul Brady's "Nobody Knows". James sang it and I thought it was brilliant. I'd never heard the song before so I said to James,

"How come you never sang that to me?"

Then Aisling butted in and said,

"Well Sarah, you're not the centre of the world".

When James heard this he stopped singing straight away and put his guitar down and he didn't sing again for the rest of the weekend. I was actually quite disappointed when I saw that he wasn't going to sing anymore and Aisling said,

"Surely that's not all you're going to sing to us Jamie?"

At the time, I didn't realise that James had stopped singing because of what Aisling had said, but he told me sometime later in our relationship when we were talking about her. James didn't like Aisling at all and he kept saying that the worst thing his friend Alex could have done was to marry her. I never really thought she was that bad but looking back at her behaviour over that weekend she was looking down on me and treating me a bit like a child.

During our first Christmas together I went over to James's house. "The Sound of Music" was on the television and I couldn't believe that James had never seen it. Mary brought some ice cream in to James and myself in the sitting room. That was when I really took to ice cream for the first time. Before that I thought that ice cream was just okay as a dessert, but for some reason after that day I grew to love it.

Before that Christmas James busked for an organisation called GROW that he was a member of, which for some reason I didn't like. Anyway, we busked outside Marks and Spencers, across from Brown Thomas on Grafton Street. James had his guitar and there were other members from GROW who sang with him. I had one of James's little drums and I did the drumming to the guitar and singing. The busking went very well and we made between 800 and 900 euro for GROW. I really enjoyed it.

As our relationship went on and as time passed, both James and myself finished off our graphic design course in ISFI and moved away from our friends there. After that I was looking for a job in graphic design but with no success, as I didn't really have any work experience at all. James didn't have a job either and he was spending his time in prayer groups and in GROW, which I didn't feel was anything to be proud of in a boyfriend. Quite early on in our relationship James mentioned to me that he didn't believe in sex before marriage. I said I was okay with that, as I'd never looked at James in that sense anyway. I think maybe one of the reasons I ended up going out with James was because he didn't want me in that way.

As neither of us had a job, we spent a lot of our time going to the cinema. I'd meet him in town on a Tuesday and a Thursday and we'd go and see a film. We'd also go to cafes and talk about nothing. James could talk and talk about nothing with no problem at all. One time when we were in the cinema together I noticed at some stage that there was something standing up in his jeans. I had a fair idea what it was, but it was totally different from previous experiences because James was just sitting there as if nothing was happening to his body at all. Anyway, I decided to find out if I was right so I tipped the palm of my hand on to it which confirmed what I was thinking. When we were leaving the cinema I said to James,

"Has your penis been erect at other times when we were in the cinema?"

James came out with, "Sorry luvvie."

I was a bit taken aback by this reply, as I would have thought that it was because of me that it was erect. I said to James,

"There's nothing to be sorry about".

Now this was a new dimension to our relationship. I was arousing James without realising it and without wanting to, but he still didn't want me and I was very happy with that. But the fact that I was arousing him was something that wasn't really fair on me because he was the one getting all the pleasure, but I guess I was getting a lot of love, I loved the way he loved me so much. All the same though, he was getting a lot of love and affection too, even if it wasn't for the right reasons. I have to say though, that I found it a bit frustrating later on in our relationship when there were quite a number of occasions that I could hardly touch him or he'd get aroused. Not once did he want me though. He loved me but he didn't want me, and I guess that's what kept us together, because I didn't really want him either and if he *had* wanted me we'd never have stayed together as long as we did.

Now, the religious side to James was kind of out of the ordinary. I mean he had a little altar in his bedroom. You see his heart was really in the church and I think he would have loved to be a priest, but I don't think he had the brains to be one. I think he wanted to get married as well though. I'd say that every time we were in town together he would have gone into a church at least once if not more. I remember noticing that James's eyes closed when he was praying, and that kind of made me consider closing my eyes too when I prayed. As I mentioned earlier in the book, when my faith was dying I decided not to bother closing my eyes when I prayed. Now my faith was restored as my epilepsy had been controlled, and when I closed my eyes to pray to God I felt closer to God than I ever had in my life. I felt God inside me very strongly, deep in my heart, which was great. Religion was the one big thing that James and myself had in common. The fact of the matter was that we didn't really have anything else in common but we still really enjoyed each other's company and James loved me to bits.

James would regularly go to confession when we were in town together. It seemed like he was always going to confession and I couldn't understand what it was that he was confessing. James was such a kind-hearted person, trying to do good for everyone else, yet he was always in confession. It was actually quite a pain, as I had to sit in the church and wait while he was waiting to confess, while he was confessing to the priest and while he was praying afterwards. There was one time when he seemed to be praying for ages after coming out of confession. When he'd finished, I said to him,

"How many Hail Mary's did you get?"

He replied, "23,000 because I was very bold".

So confession was another thing about our relationship that I hated. It was such a drag.

It became a routine that I'd go over to James's house on a Saturday night and stay over with him. Not in the same room though, I'd always sleep in his sister Gillian's room. Gillian was married to Eamon and they lived in Kildare. James had told me early on in our relationship that Gillian had lost her baby. I said to James,

"I'm very sorry to hear that".

Before Gillian became pregnant, she had slipped on a wet floor at work and had injured her back. As a result of this, the doctors told her that she'd never be able to have children. A miscarriage is awful for any mother-to-be, but losing a baby after you'd been told you couldn't have any must have been desperate. Gillian had to have the baby removed as well, which must have been awful for her.

I had, and still have, a fabulous collection of films on DVD at home and I used to bring over a film every weekend for James and myself to watch. James had a television in his room and we used to sit on his bed, James with his back up against the wall and me with my back to his chest. We'd sit there very contentedly and watch the film together. At certain times during the film James would pause it and we'd go downstairs for a break. Fred would usually be watching sport on the television and Mary would quite often be reading. The television would always be on in their house, which was quite unusual for me as in our house we only had the television on at certain times in the day.

Anyway, the two of us would be downstairs and James would be getting something to eat. James and his parents were all overweight and I'd just lost four stone in weight a year or two previously and I didn't want to put it back on again. James would go back upstairs with four slices of buttered bread with ham and cheese between them. I ended up doing the same after some time, which wouldn't have been good for my figure at all. Maybe I stayed away from the ham and cheese sandwiches initially, as I can remember going from ten stone to ten stone three and back to ten stone for quite some time at the start of our relationship, so I'd say I must have been able to refuse the food when either James or Mary offered it to me, for a while anyway.

James's room was very small and cramped, and it was a firetrap as well. I could barely count the number of plugs in his room, although I know it was somewhere in the teens. The two built-in wooden shelves on the far side of the room were full of technical equipment, hundreds of cds and other bits and bobs as well. It really was quite a mess.

James used an electric razor to shave as he was afraid of getting cut if he used a hand razor, which I thought was a bit ridiculous. He never cleaned the razor, which I thought was disgusting, although I don't know if I told him that. If I did it didn't do much good, because I hardly ever saw him clean it. He was probably just waiting for his mother to do it which I think is really sad. Twenty-nine years of age and he was getting his mother to clean his razor. He didn't take care of his hair either. His hair was long but he never brushed it, or at least I never saw him brush it. He had a hairbrush in his room but as you might guess it was full of long hairs.

James started a routine whereby the two of us would go to Mass on the Sunday morning. I think that when we started going out we used to go on Saturday evenings at seven. Before I started going out with him, I don't think I was going to Mass every Sunday, but while I was going out with James, Mass was a must.

We were waiting together at the bus stop near Trinity one day when James gave me my first taste of false hope. Now I still hadn't considered my relationship with James as being anything more than boyfriend/girlfriend and even less than that, celibate boyfriend and girlfriend. All the same, while we were waiting for the bus James said to me,

"It will probably be about seven years before I can support you".

When I heard this first I didn't think much of it, but James had said it and the idea of him supporting me made me presume or hope to have a house with him. James was giving me false hope of things I'd given up hoping for already . . . my dream family of four children. I'd given up on this a long time ago, and now James—the man without a job and on disability allowance—was making me hope for something that deep down I knew I was never going to get.

We were still meeting up during the week and going to see film after film and when the latest "Star Wars" was coming out, James was preparing me for it and educating me about the previous Star Wars films. James loved "Star Wars—it was his favourite film whereas I'd never taken to it and I hadn't watched one of them in full. In the end, though, I actually quite enjoyed it.

Another thing that really embarrassed me about James was when he'd get his father to drive us places. There were times when we'd be standing at the bus stop in town and James would invite me over to his house out of the blue. I hadn't been keeping spare tablets in my bag at the time and when I didn't have the tablets James said that he'd ask his dad to drive us over to my house to get them. There was nothing I could do about this, and the fact that James didn't drive and probably never would was really getting on my nerves. It made me feel kind of helpless in a way.

What's coming back to me now is the first time I mentioned something to my parents about James. When I said to my parents,

"I have a boyfriend",

Dad immediately said to me,

"What kind of education does he have?"

This happened early on in our relationship and I hadn't thought about education at all. I hadn't a clue what kind of education James had and I really didn't care either. I was glad to be rid of education to be honest with you. That's all my life had been in the past, and now I had someone to share my past with, someone who would listen to what I'd gone through and console me by telling me something that he'd gone through that was hard for him.

Anyway, after Dad had asked about James's education I went to James and I asked him. James told me that he left secondary school after his Junior Cert. When I heard that I knew it wasn't good. Dad certainly wasn't going to be happy about that. I told Mum and Dad that James had left school after his Junior Cert and that he had depression. On hearing this Dad definitely didn't approve of James. Dad had never approved of him and I think the idea of the possibility of me having James's child was killing him. I'm sure that Dad didn't want to be putting up with James's baby waking him in the middle of the night. The thing is though, James and Mum and Dad were running away with my relationship. I had never thought of marrying James or sleeping with him, but these things were coming up on both sides. My parents were presuming that I was sleeping with James, and he was planning on marrying me, and these two things were killing me.

When I first mentioned going over to stay with James Mum said,

"We'd better get you on the pill".

I paid no attention to this because I knew I didn't need to be on the pill. Dad didn't want me staying overnight with James, but I said to my parents,

"You can't stop me".

Dad said, "We can't stop you".

I knew they were worried that I'd get pregnant but I knew that I definitely wouldn't get pregnant. At some stage in the conversation I said to my parents,

"If I get pregnant you can kill me!!"

Mum said, "We can't kill you Sarah, you're ours".

Then Dad said to me, "If you get pregnant don't come home".

I said "Okay".

I actually think that Dad regretted saying that in the end but we never talked about it again. Dad was losing me because he thought I was going to sleep with James.

There were occasions after that when my Dad in particular ended up bringing me to tears. There were times that I'd burst out crying because Dad was trying to split James and myself up. All I wanted was a friend in James, but all I was getting from my parents was disappointment in James and them looking down on him. As long as I was going out with James I felt I was letting my parents down. I remember comparing myself to Princess Fiona in the film SHREK 2, when she's having an awful time introducing her new husband to her parents. What's gas is that now I relate my relationship with Alex to the first film SHREK—the part where Fiona and Shrek go their separate ways, but they really want to be with each other.

Sometime after Mum and Dad had met James I was talking to them in the kitchen and to try and split us up Mum said to me,

"Sarah, we think that James is a bit simple".

This made me burst into tears again probably because I thought they could be right. I mean I was better than James at an awful lot of things. We were playing draughts one time and every game that we played I won, so we ended up not playing draughts any more. I'd always beat James at pool too, so we didn't play much pool either. James's English was pathetic and that was something I hated.

Music was the one thing that James was good at but he still wasn't good enough to make a living out of it but I'll give him something, he definitely tried. One time he sent one of his own songs into a competition for the Eurovision, but I was pretty sure he wasn't going to get in. It was around that time that I decided to look at engagement rings in a jeweller's one day, knowing that there wasn't much of a chance that I was ever going to get one. When James saw me looking at them he said to me,

"If I get chosen for the Eurovision I'll be able to buy you all of them".

This was James giving me false hope again. I started hoping that he *would* get chosen but just like I'd presumed, he didn't.

The first time I went to a concert with James was when we went to see Bob Dylan in Nolan Park in Kilkenny. We both agreed that it was a very bad concert. There was hardly any atmosphere at all. We did make the best of our trip though. We had paid for a B & B for the weekend and we had a great time exploring Kilkenny. It's such a lovely place. I remember being particularly impressed by the selection of ice cream in the restaurants.

James used to phone me every day and there were times when he'd be talking and I'd be sick of listening to him going on and on about nothing in particular. Anyway, one day he phoned me, and he told me something heartbreaking. He told me that he'd found out that he had a disability called dyscalculia and that it was genetic. He said that it was a problem with Maths. When I finished on the phone with him I went on to the internet and googled it. My heart sank when I saw what a serious and debilitating disability it was. People with dyscalculia can't drive unless they really want to, and they can't dance as they can't tell their left from their right. Early on in our relationship, I bought James a really expensive watch because I noticed that he didn't have one. He never wore it and that was because he couldn't tell the time, but he never told me that. Dyscalculia was a desperate disability to have and the fact that it was genetic made it even worse.

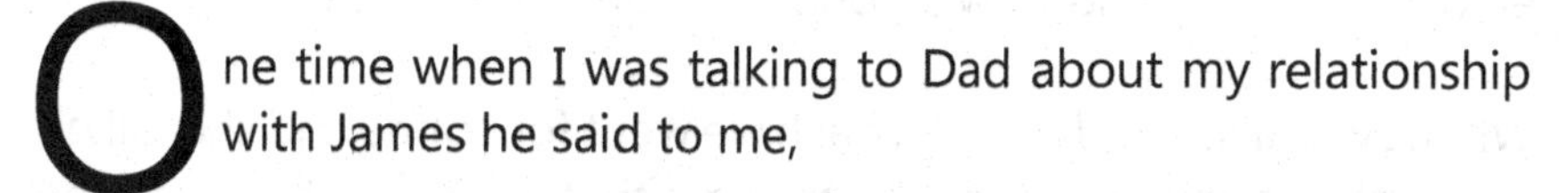

One time when I was talking to Dad about my relationship with James he said to me,

"You'll never have a house".

This had quite an effect on me as deep down I knew that Dad was right, but still James was giving me the impression that that was where our relationship was going. Then when James and myself were talking one day, at some stage I came out with,

"I always wanted four children".

I didn't mean that I wanted to have four children with James, but as I mentioned earlier in the book that was what I dreamt of when I was a child. James went home and actually said to his mother,

"She wants four children".

I really hated James's relationship with his mother. After that, Mary, James's mother, said to me a few times,

"I don't think he'll be having many children".

This got on my nerves but I didn't say anything. All the same I was thinking to myself, *'Does she think I'm stupid? It's quite obvious that he's not going to have any children, he can't even tell his left from his right and he's a priest at heart'.*

Since neither James nor myself were working that was something we needed to try and rectify. James had heard that you could get help from a job coach but you had to go on to a waiting list, so we both put our names on the waiting list in our own areas. James got a job coach first, and she worked with James to help him to find work. He ended up getting a job three days a week in some kind of social home for elderly people and people in wheelchairs. He had to help these people with their toilet activities, and he also had to entertain them, though I'm sure that was the part of the job he would have enjoyed. He also had to walk one particular man home.

When I was allocated my job coach we went for coffee and she talked to me about what she did. She told me that she'd meet up with me and we'd work together on getting a job, but she also told me to think about other options apart from work in graphic design, which was what I was doing. One day I mentioned to her that I'd always dreamt of working with children but that because I had epilepsy I felt it would be out of the question. She said that as my epilepsy was now under control we could look into the possibility of working with children. I found a course in Montessori and Childcare in Liberties College off Patrick Street in the city centre. All I needed to apply for a place was a Leaving Cert, which I had, and two references. I also had to get a note from my doctor saying that my epilepsy was under control.

I had no problem getting the note from my doctor, so the next thing was the references. I decided I'd go and see my friend Susan up the road. I had helped Susan to take care of her four children while Susan was on her ten-year career break, and I'd spent a lot of time with them. I had helped them do their homework, I had motivated them to learn, and I'd helped them to learn to walk. I had a ball while I was doing it and it was one of the few things I enjoyed in my teen years. Susan gave me a lovely reference, which was great, so I was halfway there. Then I approached the manager of the course I did with ISFI, and with a lot of persuasion and perseverance I got quite a good reference from him as well.

One weekend around this time Mary, James's mother suggested that I do some voluntary work for a crèche. I ended up doing three hours on a Monday morning in a Montessori school nearby. I really enjoyed myself there and when I was finished they gave me a lovely reference. Now I had three good references and I was very confident that I'd get in to the two-year course in Montessori and Childcare. A good bit of my confidence had come from my dad. I remember Dad saying to me in total confidence,

"You'll get in", and as I've said earlier in the book my dad was very rarely wrong about anything he said. Shortly after an interview in Liberties College I got a letter from them saying that I'd been accepted. I took to the course straight away and I loved it. I spent three days a week in the college and the other two days on work experience in a crèche.

At this stage in my life, I wasn't talking to my dad as much as I used to, as our relationship had totally changed since I'd started going out with James. I wasn't Daddy's little girl anymore. I also felt that I'd let my dad down by having James as my boyfriend. Anyway, Dad and myself were in the kitchen one day and for some reason I said to him,

"You'll be proud of me".

My dad immediately replied,

"Sarah, I'm always proud of you".

This touched my heart and made me very happy.

James and myself were still going out and we were quite happy with the way things were, but there were still occasions when I'd burst out crying. One Sunday on the way to Mass—I don't know exactly what I said to James to provoke this—but James said to me,

"I don't think we'll have a house", or something like that.

I'm not sure how I reacted to this when he said it first, but what I remember very clearly is how I was in the church. Tears started pouring down my face, and I turned to get James's attention and then we both walked out of the church. Then I said to James,

"Dad said to me that we'd never have a house".

James's reply to this was,

"Oh, I didn't know he said that".

That was one of the worst times where James had built me up to hope for something we both knew wasn't going to happen, and then he smashed my hopes to bits.

The fact that James made me laugh so much was one of the things that kept us together. I can remember going into hat shops a lot and James would try on hat after hat and I'd be laughing and laughing at him. There were two other things about James that I didn't like but that couldn't break us up. He snored. He snored so loud that I could hear him in the other room through the wall. And something even worse was the way he'd let out a scream in the middle of the night and make me jump in my bed in the room next door. He'd be having a nightmare or something and he'd scream so loud that I'd be worried that he'd give me a heart attack some night with the fright.

The first thing James bought me that I really loved was a towelling dressing gown. It was a beautiful royal blue colour and it had a lovely blue ribbon going along the edge of it. I still have it and I love it. He used to buy me loads of teddy bears and he bought flowers for me quite often. I remember that one time he got flowers delivered to me, which I'd say he got his mother to help him with, because I couldn't see James knowing how to do it himself. What happened was that I had a seizure in bed early in the morning. I'd been free of seizures for nearly a year, and this was the first one I'd had since I went on to my new medication and since I started going out with James. When I came downstairs and was coming back to myself, I saw a lovely big bouquet of flowers waiting for me and it had a lovely little card in it with a message for me. I wasn't fully myself so Mum took care of them.

James was always spending money on me. He still loved me so much. One night when I was on the phone to him I said,

"If I could have all the money in the world or have your hair cut, I'd choose for your hair to be cut".

I hated the fact that James had long hair, but he loved me so much that he got it cut for me.

We were really quite a romantic couple. We'd give each other cards and we'd go out for meals all the time together. We'd go to the cinema together at least once a week, we'd go to plays and concerts and there were a couple of times when we went on a week's holiday in the Talbot Hotel in Wexford, which we loved. We'd go to the gym and we'd swim in the pool. James was pretty bad at swimming of course. As usual, I was better than he was, and there was no chance of us having a race because he didn't like getting water in his mouth. We really enjoyed the breakfast in the hotel because they had such a huge selection of food. I'd always go for the Mediterranean breakfast. We also enjoyed going out for meals in Wexford.

One of the weeks we were on holidays in Wexford we went to the cinema three times. The two films I remember were '*Hancock*' with Will Smith and '*Mamma Mia*' with Meryl Streep. We'd get a taxi to the cinema and back to the hotel again. There was one time when we couldn't get a taxi after the film—I can't remember why exactly. It might have been that we didn't have the money with us or it might have had something to do with not having our mobile phones. The cinema was a few miles outside the town, and we ended up walking all the way back to the Talbot Hotel. I remember being quite nervous walking along the side of the road, not having a clue where I was going, and thinking to myself that we could have been walking towards Waterford instead. But we got back in the end and I actually remember it as something quite exciting that happened in our relationship.

I'd been going over to James's house for quite some time now and I was really getting to know his family. His dad, Fred was always watching sport on the television and I can remember watching snooker with him one night. I really enjoy watching snooker as I played a lot of pool and snooker as a child, or at least I watched Dad and Peter play together so I was around it a lot. They would have been watching it on television when I was growing up, and they would have explained all the rules to me. I got to know James's sister Gillian and her husband Eamon quite well too. They were big into building houses and they were building a huge house in Kildare, which they were going to sell when they had it finished. Gillian became pregnant at some stage during our relationship and had a baby boy, who they named Ray.

James and his parents had kept birds throughout all of James's life. James was obsessed with birds if you ask me. He'd go out into the back garden with slices of bread and spend what seemed like ages breaking up the bread and throwing it down on to the grass for the birds. He'd be doing this while I was standing inside, which I didn't like. Never once did he offer me a slice of bread and invite me out into the garden to feed the birds with him. James would also spend ages playing with his pet bird, and this got on my nerves too.

I remember Mary, James's mother saying that the FETAC awards that James got from the graphic design course where the two of us met were a waste of paper. I thought this was an awful thing to say. Mary was a real nag, and she'd always be nagging James to do things. I can't remember exactly what she'd be telling him to do but their relationship was totally different from Peter and Mum's relationship. Mum wasn't like that at all and she'd rarely tell Peter to do something, though I don't know whether this was a good thing or a bad thing. Since Mary was nagging James to do things I started going in the same direction. Mary kind of turned me into someone I wasn't, and I started not to like who I was without realising it.

I remember something else that happened to make me not like who I was. James and myself would be in church on Sunday and a lot of the time the singing in the church wasn't that good. I wouldn't really recognise it because I can't sing myself, but James would definitely notice if they were singing off key. Anyway, while they were singing I'd notice James holding back laughter and he looked so funny. So then I started laughing at the singers or holding back laughter, but I was only doing this because of James, and inside I really hated what I was doing, but I have to say I did enjoy it all the same.

Another thing I didn't like about James was his teeth, and especially his gums. James had very dark red gums and his teeth didn't look healthy at all. He didn't go to the dentist once during the five years while we were going out. I'd rarely see him looking in the mirror either. I don't think he really cared that much about his appearance.

I can remember one time when James gave me a kiss that I loved. It was a Saturday morning and I'd stayed over in his house on the Friday night. I'd got up early on the Saturday and I was downstairs at their dining room table reading a Montessori book. Just after he got up and came downstairs, James came over to me and gave me an unexpected kiss on the cheek. I loved it. I always found that a kiss on the cheek or a kiss on the hand was a great way of telling someone that you love them. This was one of the rare occasions that I actually got a kiss on the cheek. I'd often kiss James on the hand and he'd always return my kiss by kissing me on the hand.

I went to the zoo quite a few times with James as he lived near enough to the Phoenix Park. This was great, because I'd hardly ever been in the zoo before I started going out with him. We had great fun looking at all the animals together. We hired out bicycles as well and cycled around the park together and looked at all the deer.

Something I found very unusual about James's family, and in particular James and his dad, was that they hated mayonnaise. I'd never met anybody who didn't like mayonnaise. James's dad hated mayonnaise so much that he'd start brushing his tongue with a toothbrush if he ate something with mayonnaise on it, and he'd be washing his mouth out big time. James was limited enough in what he'd eat as well. He wouldn't eat fish for instance because he'd be afraid he'd choke. He also wouldn't really eat anything with a sauce on it. I don't think he'd ever ordered a pizza before he met me, because the first time we ordered a pizza in his house, James and/or his mother set the table with plates, knives and forks . . . the things you don't need when you order pizza as you eat it out of the box with your hands.

While I was going out with James I went to a number of funerals. The first was the funeral of my dad's stepmother Lily. I think Lily knew when she was leaving the world as just before she died, she said something like,

"I think he's taking me now".

Mum, Dad, Peter and myself went down to Tipperary for the funeral and we met up with all of our relations to say goodbye to Lily.

James used to sing to me a lot, and a routine developed of him serenading me before I went to sleep. He had music books with the lyrics of so many songs. He also used to print out the lyrics of certain songs off the computer. One of the songs he loved singing to me was Lionel Richie's "Hello". I'd ask him to sing "Desperado" to me, and "Annie's Song". One day we were looking at the lyrics of the songs together and we noticed a lot of similarities between "Desperado" and "Annie's Song", which we actually found quite amazing.

I'd be on at James to go busking all the time and sometimes he said he would but he never did. The one time he did, he actually brought a music stand with him and read the lyrics while he sang, which I actually found quite embarrassing. Yet again, James was embarrassing me. I don't know whether it was that he couldn't learn the lyrics of songs because of his dyscalculia disability, or that he just couldn't be bothered, but he hardly tried at all to learn off songs. I even tried to help him to learn the words of "Annie's Song" which are very simple, but he just didn't seem to be able to remember the lyrics at all, which I found quite weird. All that "Annie's Song" consisted of was two short verses and James didn't seem to be able for it.

Chapter 34

One weekend when I was over in James's I got a call from my mum. She had phoned me to let me know that my dad had had a stroke while they were down in Wexford. Dad was fully conscious but he couldn't walk or use his right arm. After about a week, Dad was moved up to Tallaght hospital in Dublin near where we live.

I was just starting my Montessori and Childcare course at the time and I was doing two days work experience in a crèche nearby. I was also spending three days a week in college and I was getting to know a lot of girls who were all around twenty years of age. There was just one other mature student about the same age as me. They were all lovely and we formed a very nice class.

James and his family were very supportive when my dad was in hospital. James's dad gave me a lift to the hospital quite a number of times, although the fact that James didn't drive was getting to me and I'd always be suggesting to him that he should learn how to drive. At the time I didn't realise how bad he was at even just knowing his left and right.

Dad wasn't long in Tallaght hospital when he got pneumonia and ended up in a coma in intensive care. We had great support from family members as well as from dad's siblings and their spouses. Some of my cousins were there as well. We'd take turns going in to see Dad as there could only be two people in with him at a time. The rest of us waited in a little room outside the intensive care unit.

James was there as well taking care of me and giving me loads of support.

After some time Dad pulled through, but now he had a speech valve and he was getting dialysis. Dad also had MRSA, and he was so overweight that the chances of him walking again were very slim. As time passed, Dad ended up getting physiotherapy just to help him sit up straight on his own. In the end, what actually killed my dad was a lump of phlegm that got caught in his throat. His heart stopped and the doctors and nurses couldn't get it going for a few minutes, so Dad's brain had been without oxygen for quite some time. The doctor said that he'd never seen so many complications in a stroke patient before.

When my dad died I just went with the flow of things. I never cried because I had shed all of those tears when Dad was painfully letting me go to James. In a way, James really made losing my dad a lot easier. You could say it was a more gentle way of losing someone you really loved. When I lost my dad for James a couple of years previously my dad was still there. I could see him and I could talk to him. Now, if my dad had got a stroke and died within months, before I was going out with James, I would have been in bits. But James was there for me when Dad died and he was full of support and love and he took great care of me. I have to say that when I was going out with James, I'd thank God every Sunday at Mass for the two big things that had changed my life. I'd thank God for James, and for the medication Keppra, which gave me a new outlook on life. I said to Mum at some stage,

"Mum, I got three of my dreams coming true around the same time . . . My epilepsy under control, a man to love, and to be able to work with children".

After my Dad died, when we were getting the house ready for people to come back to after the removal, I decided to get out some photographs of Dad. I also got big A1 sheets of black paper out of my portfolio. I went through loads of photographs with Dad in them and I stuck them down on the black paper. I had one page where the photos were mainly black and white. I had different sheets of paper for the different stages of his life—photographs of when he was a baby and then a young boy down in Waterford. I had about four or five sheets altogether and I stuck them up on the walls around the house for people to look at after the removal. This was my artistic side coming out.

My Dad was cremated, and we had a special get-together for a scattering of the ashes down at Blackwater beach. I had great fun designing an invitation to send out to all the people we were going to invite to the ceremony, which was a very enjoyable celebration. We had a friend of ours who's a priest say a few words at the river on the beach flowing into the sea. Then Mum, Peter, five of Dad's siblings and myself were each given a portion of my dad's ashes which had been put into identical shells which Mum had for presentation of certain fish starters. After the priest had said his piece we were all invited to scatter the ashes in the river.

I was the first person to walk into the river as I was in flip flops and a skirt so I was all set. I scattered my ashes and then walked out of the river. My uncles had to take off their shoes and roll up their trousers so it was a few minutes more before all the ashes were scattered. After the ceremony we all headed back to the new house in Garryvadden to have something to eat and to just enjoy each other's company. My dad's cousin's husband, who's dead now God rest his soul, was a singer and he had brought his guitar with him. James had his guitar with him too, along with a lot of books with the lyrics of different songs. The two of them brought their stuff into the sunroom and a big group of us followed them in and we had a lovely singsong.

That was only half of my dad's ashes though. The other half were in a lovely small wooden casket in the shape of a coffin, and we had another special Mass and we placed the ashes in his parents' grave in Dungarvan where my dad was from. My uncle Tadhg, my dad's brother-in-law, also died while I was going out with James and he had previously been buried in that grave. So, it's a very special grave. After all of this was over it was time to make the memorial card. I decided I'd design it and that it would be a memorial bookmark. It was a mix of the colours green, yellow, and brown and there was a bit of turquoise in there as well. On one side I had the top of a lovely photo of Dad, which was taken while we were on holiday in Sicily. I also had a photo of a honeybee on a dandelion down at the bottom. Just above the bee, I had placed the text, "He has gone no further from us than to God and God is very near", which I thought was nice. On the other side I had three photos. One was of Dad when he was in his teens, one when he was in his late twenties and one when he was in his thirties. I also had another prayer typed out curving around the photos. I have to say I really enjoyed designing it.

I was still going to college through all of this and I was learning about Maria Montessori and her method of teaching children. It was really quite interesting learning about all of her materials and how they benefit the child. The thing is though in Ireland anyway, there are very few real Montessori schools, which is a terrible pity because children with special needs would particularly benefit from going to a Montessori school. Most of the "Montessori" schools in Dublin seem to me to be just crèches with the name Montessori to make them sound better. I'm not saying that these crèches aren't good for the children, I'm sure they are. It's just that I don't like the way that, in my experience anyway, the children are just playing with the Montessori materials rather than actually being taught using the materials.

All the same though, I was still enjoying the course. I'd come home after college and I'd work on my files for the different sections of Montessori. In first year we learned about "Practical Life". This was a section where the children learn to do things like pouring or spooning, for example, and they'd learn in stages. The first step would be pouring pasta and when the child had mastered pouring pasta they'd be introduced to pouring rice. Then after a while, they'd finally be introduced to pouring water. Then there was the Montessori section called "Sensorial", where the children work with the Montessori materials designed to develop the child's senses. One of the materials in the Sensorial section that I particularly liked was the red rods. The red rods were wooden, like most of

Montessori's materials which were all made from natural materials. These rectangular red rods were like ten different-sized wooden poles, the smallest being about four inches long and the longest being ten times the size of the smallest.

When I went on work experience I hated watching the children use these red rods as swords and playing sword fights with each other. These rods had so much more to offer than that. There was one exercise in particular that I managed to do with the whole group of children in the Montessori classroom. It was called "the maze". This is where you create a maze using the red rods. When the maze is built, each child gets a turn walking one foot in front of the other, through a square maze with a gap between the rods of about five inches. The children loved it.

Now that Dad was gone, Mum needed someone to come down to Wexford with her so she invited James and myself down. Mum would be driving, I'd be in the front passenger seat, and James would be in the back seat with Sandy.

Our home in Garryvadden was totally different now. Dad had managed to build a fabulous new house before he died. He'd replaced the gravel driveway with smooth tarmac, and there was a huge big area of lawn where there used to be just soil and weeds. I think the best feature of the house was the island in the middle of the kitchen with two or three stools around it. I think the compost bin was underneath it as well as I think Dad had planned to chop the vegetables on the island so he could put the peelings etc. into the bin underneath. There was a fabulous wheelchair-friendly bathroom, lovely and big. There were three bedrooms downstairs and a lovely wooden stairs that led up to another two rooms. It really is a fabulous house.

Chapter 35

There was very little conversation between James and myself anytime we were down in Garryvadden. I guess I just didn't feel comfortable, as the place just wasn't James at all. I was totally at home there, because it's my second home and it's part of who I am. It was all new to James though, and I remember him being fascinated by cows coming up to him at the gate onto the field across the road. I had experienced that growing up so it was nothing new to me. James would be standing at the gate and I'd just want to be walking down the lane. He'd stop at the field with a few horses in it too and just stand there, and I'd be getting annoyed because I just wanted to continue walking. This was another example of James really turning me into someone I didn't like. I didn't like who I was when I was with James but I never said that to anybody.

James's back became a problem early on in our relationship and the fact that he was going on about his back really got on my nerves as well, but I guess that wasn't his fault so it didn't break us up. Of course I couldn't end the relationship . . . I just didn't have it in me. James loved me so much that it was controlling me, controlling who I was and who I was becoming.

All the same, the fact of the matter is, I wasn't anybody before I started going out with James. I didn't have the confidence to say what I liked and to make choices for myself. James actually helped me find myself. Johnny Depp for instance, I didn't even like, never mind love, before I started going out with James. I didn't like any actor in particular, and I would have judged films on the storyline and not the acting. That was something very different between Dad and myself. I'd watch the films for the storyline whereas Dad would be totally focused on the actors, so focused in fact, that he'd hardly relate to the characters at all. But I have to say fair play to Johnny Depp and little Freddie Highmore in the film "Finding Neverland". I'll never forget when I was watching that film with my Dad. At the end of the film, Dad was actually totally drawn in to the character, the little boy that was acted by Freddie Highmore. In the film, Johnny Depp, who plays the part of J M Barrie is sitting on a bench with the little boy whose name is Peter. Peter is in tears and Dad related to Peter, and I can remember him saying something like, "the poor little lad". Then I saw Dad kind of realise that, oh, yea he's just an actor. It was funny really.

It was through buying things for me, dvds for example, that James helped me find who I was. "*Pirates of the Caribbean: The Curse of the Black Pearl*" and "*Finding Neverland*", were two films that I went to see in the cinema before I started going out with James but that I didn't take to. All the same, somehow, James bought them for me and now I love both films and I love Johnny Depp.

James also helped me in the area of music. One time I told him about a cd of Elton John's love songs I had which was broken, and he went out and bought me a new one. He often used to buy me cds, which I'd listen to and then talk to him about. I would have bought cds in the past, probably during my teen years but, like the films, I'd never have known anything about the singer or the band. James educated me in that way as well, although I think part of all of this was because my epilepsy was under control and I had more independence and my confidence was growing.

It was while I was going out with James that I ended up getting a brace for my teeth. Mum had been going on at me about it but I wasn't very keen on the idea. Then one day she said to me,

"Sarah, if you get a brace I'll pay for it".

How could I resist? So I went to the dentist and he sent me to an orthodontist who lived nearby. She sent me back to the dentist to get four teeth pulled out. Then she put on the brace and told me what I could and couldn't eat. She also gave me special wax to put on the brace if it was rubbing off my mouth. It really was quite painful.

When I was down in Garryvadden with Mum and James the three of us would go to Blackwater beach and I'd go down to the sea to skim stones. I couldn't believe it when James said he couldn't skim stones and when he basically walked away from me as if he didn't care. On other occasions, James and myself went to the beach with my aunt Sylvia and my two cousins Niamh and Maeve, and once we brought a kite with us. I'd bought a really good kite in the art and hobby shop and we'd chosen a nice windy day to go and fly it. We had no trouble at all getting it in the air and once it was up there I began to get bored and feel like I had nothing to do. That was when I realised that the time you spend trying to get the kite in the air can actually be more fun than when the kite is actually up in the air.

Sometimes when I was with James it felt like being with a child, as I had to keep watching him to see if he was going about doing something in the correct way. One day when we were finished flying the kite, my aunt and my two cousins started making their way off the beach heading for the car. James had the kite which was still in the air. He started following us up through the dunes and down the lane. It hadn't occurred to him that he should have taken the kite down out of the air before walking off the beach. In the end, the kite got caught in a bush and we had to leave it there. It was this kind of incident that would make me feel that James had no sense at all. Maybe he'd never flown a kite before, I don't know.

I had now started the second year of my Montessori course and we were learning Montessori Maths, which I loved. There were so many materials we could use to teach the children their numbers and other things too. There were the sandpaper numbers to start with. These were small, green square sheets of wood, each of which had one of the numbers from zero to nine on it in sandpaper. The child would be taught to slide their two forefingers along the sandpaper and they'd be introduced to the number as well. There was what we called the three-period lesson which was used in Sensorial and in Montessori Language as well. It goes like this, "This is one, one". This is two, two". Then you'd say to the child, "Show me one", "show me two", and the child would point to the numbers. The third period is, "What's this?", where the child would tell you what number it is. This method of teaching was used to teach the children their letters—made of sandpaper—and their colours as well.

There are number rods in Montessori Maths as well. They're very similar to the red rods from the Sensorial section that I described earlier, only this time they're painted blue and red instead of just red. Well, the first one is just plain red but as they the longer you have blue and red, then you have blue, red and blue. Then you have blue, red, blue, red and so on up as far as ten. The three-period method is used here as well and this exercise should be presented to the child before the sandpaper numbers, in order to introduce him or her to the sound of the numbers. After they've mastered the sound, they are then introduced to the image of the numbers using little wooden plates with the number on them in black. The child then has to match up the rod with the number.

Another exercise in Montessori Maths that I loved was called "the spindle box", which was used to introduce the child to zero. The spindle box was a large wooden box divided into ten sections which were numbered in black from zero to nine. There was a big bundle of spindles, which were basically like little sticks of wood about six inches long. The child had to fill each section of the box with the number of sticks that matched the number printed in that section. When this was done correctly, there would be no spindles left for the section that had the number zero printed in it. This showed the child that zero means nothing. I loved Montessori Maths. I think it was my favourite of all of the modules we had to do. My graphic design skills came in very handy when it came to illustrating my file. In fact, the illustrations were so good that the teacher said I could publish it but I never did.

I remember going down to visit James's nephew Ray when he was about a year old. His parents, Gillian and Eamon, had a whole room full of toys for him. He had so many toys that you couldn't count them. He was also allowed to race around the huge house they had in his walker. Even then I could see that he was spoilt. Then when he got older and he was up in Dublin with us, I just couldn't help but notice that Gillian and Eamon had very little control over him. I really found it strange being around Ray as he didn't seem to take to me like all the other children I'd been around. One day when I arrived home from James's house I started talking to Mum about Ray and I said to her,

"He's the most unsociable child I've ever been around".

Mum said to me,

"He wouldn't be autistic would he?"

I was a bit taken aback by this as it would never have crossed my mind, but I went and got my Childcare book and looked up autism.

My heart sank when I read through the characteristics to look out for in an autistic child. As I read through them, it seemed as if, one after the other, they matched perfectly the way that Ray was behaving, certainly around me anyway. For example, lack of awareness of other people. Ray basically totally ignored me while I was around him, which seemed very unusual to me as children normally relate and come to me very quickly. Some of the other traits he seemed to have were lack of eye-to-eye contact, and delayed speech. It looked as if he had special skills too, another trait. Ray really took to a calculator and he was better at maths than James was. It was awful. I just kept relating these characteristics to Ray and from that day on, Ray was autistic in my opinion. Gillian and Eamon didn't seem to think there was anything wrong with Ray at all which kind of upset me a bit, because I felt that the longer he went without being diagnosed, the harder it might be to try to correct.

Maybe I should have said something to Gillian, I don't know, but I just didn't have it in me. I never related to Gillian and Eamon very well. I don't know why, but I was never really able to open up very well, in particular to Gillian. I used to talk to James all the time about Ray having autism but he didn't really say anything to anyone about it.

Chapter 36

A while after this, James's dad got pancreatic cancer. He was treated with chemotherapy and he suffered very bad side-effects. I think James's Dad died within months of being diagnosed with cancer, which was very sad, but I have to say James coped very well. Now James had to get a suit to wear to the funeral. James was thirty-one or thirty two years of age when he got his first suit and his mother went with him to buy it. It's these kinds of things that show that James was such a child. He hardly seemed to be able to do anything himself.

On James's thirty-third birthday I broke down in tears once again. I didn't mean it to happen on his birthday, it just did. I mean you can't control these things really. We were in Easons café off O'Connell Street and we were talking over coffee. I don't know what happened exactly, but James must have said something to me that I didn't like because I remember getting up off my seat, grabbing my bags and starting to walk away from him. When I did this, James jumped up off his seat and grabbed my arm and got me to sit back down again. Whatever was going on between us was too much for me to take, and I felt totally trapped. I couldn't escape this relationship and it was killing me. I put my head down on the table in Easons and I burst out crying.

I think this incident really affected James, as he brought it up a number of times towards the end of our relationship. I think the fact that it happened on his birthday was a big part of it. All the same, James still had me as his girlfriend and he was spending loads of money on me. I think he was trying to buy my love. I won't go into everything he bought for me but he bought me such fabulous stuff that even now, nearly two years after we broke up, I still have quite a few things he gave me, and they're so good I don't know how I'm going to get rid of them. A lovely hi-fi system for example, I won't be able to get rid of that until it breaks. Even then, if and when it does break, how am I going to go about getting rid of it?

Gillian and Eamon had another baby while I was going out with James, another boy who they named Derek, and another nephew for James. Shortly before Derek's first birthday, James and myself were invited down to Kerry to stay with Gillian and Eamon, who had moved there from Kildare and were renting a big house there. It wasn't the most fantastic holiday, but it wasn't really a bad holiday either, it's just I guess I felt kind of trapped as usual. I felt I couldn't open up to Gillian and Eamon for some reason. I was totally focused on Ray yet again but I couldn't say anything about it to Gillian and Eamon, because I was afraid of how they'd react. I kept going on about it to James when we were alone though. James noticed something about Ray that weekend. He told me that he thought the way Ray said goodnight was very unusual. Apparently, Ray had just walked over towards Eamon a bit and then lowered his head slightly, and that was how he said goodnight. That was the first time James realised that I could be right about the autism.

When we were back in James's house in Dublin with his mum, the three of us were sitting at the dining room table. At one stage while we were talking, I came out with,

"When we were in love . . ."

I'm not sure exactly why I said that, but Mary immediately replied,

"Are you not in love now?"

James came in with "yes" straight away, but I just said,

"Well, it's kind of a hands-off love".

This incident gave Mary the final tool to work with on breaking the two of us up. James had been saying things recently to me like,

"What do you want?" or "Sarah, I love you for my life".

I didn't really respond to either of the things he said, and certainly not to, "I love you for my life".

I was finally beginning to separate from James but I didn't actually know it.

After I'd gone home I got a phone call from James. He was saying that he'd been defending me because Gillian was saying that I wasn't pulling my weight. He was going on big time about him defending me, but it didn't mean anything to me because I felt like I had been defending James a lot since we started going out. I wasn't sure what to say, I mean I was the guest, what was I supposed to be doing? So I said to James,

"Then we won't go down to them again".

James said, "What?"

Then he said, "I'll phone you again tomorrow".

That was the shortest phone call I had ever had with James.

The following morning when I was in bed I got another phone call from James. He was saying that he thought we should break up. He told me that he'd told his mum what I'd been saying about the autism and that she'd said that was a doctor's decision. He also said, "I love Ray", which I didn't like because that suggested that *I* didn't love Ray, and the idea of me not loving a child is not on. I love children. I love all children, even if people call them brats, I love them all. As usual though, I didn't say this to James but it did annoy me. James also said,

"If you really loved me . . ." I'm not sure in what context he said that, but I remember him saying it. He also mentioned,

"We can still be friends".

I replied, "I don't know if I could do that".

He told me he was in bits during the night, and that was when I realised that it was his mother breaking us up. His mother was basically saying, '*How dare anyone call my grandson autistic, she's not going to be part of this family*'. I mentioned the fact that he was breaking us up over the phone and he said,

"I was afraid you'd break down".

I didn't say anything to that, but I guess I thought to myself that deep down I wanted this to happen. Mary and Ray had broken us up and I felt it was a blessing in disguise.

After I'd broken up with James, I went down to Wexford with my mother to make a fresh start. I was quite upset for a day or two, particularly if I heard a song on the radio that James had sung to me a lot. All the same, I always knew deep down that our relationship was going nowhere, so I got over him pretty quickly. To be honest, I was more upset from worrying about him than actually not having him in my life anymore.

Before we broke up we'd bought tickets to go and see Elton John in the O2 at the start of November, so that was occupying my mind a lot. I wasn't going to phone James about it, as I was still annoyed about what he'd said to me about not loving Ray, and I had no intention of bringing it up with him. I had the tickets in my possession so I was wondering what I should do with them. I was thinking to myself, if James doesn't contact me about them maybe I'll end up going to the concert with someone else. I'd been listening to a lot of Elton John's music over the past three months and I was really enjoying it.

After staying a couple of nights in Wexford, Mum and myself headed over to my aunt, Rose's house in Dungarvan. We were on our way to a party in Tralee and it was an opportunity to stay in Dungarvan. As usual, I had a great night's sleep and what made it even better was that I had a fabulous dream about Johnny Depp. I was in such good form when I got up. I was thinking to myself, I don't need James in my life anymore. We stayed for one night in my aunt's house and then headed on our way to Tralee. When we got to Tralee we checked into the hotel and then we went shopping, as I needed a dress for the party. That night after my mother had gone to bed I headed downstairs to the lounge, found a nice table and sat down at it. I caught the eye of one of the bar staff and ordered a hot chocolate.

There was a nice, handsome man playing the piano just across the room a little bit away from me. I really enjoyed sitting there drinking my hot chocolate and listening to him playing beautiful music. After a while, I decided to go over to him, and I said to him,

"Do you play Elton John?"

He replied, "What do you want?"

I replied, "Well, I love Nikita".

He said, "I'll play that for YOU".

I went back to my seat and ordered another hot chocolate. I was in my element sitting there listening to him play my favourite song and enjoying my hot chocolate at the same time. When I was finished I stood up, and as I was leaving, I said to the pianist,

"Thank you, that was beautiful".

As I was heading to bed I was thinking to myself, wow, imagine if I could go and see Elton John with him, and even though I was pretty sure it wasn't going to happen, it was still very enjoyable just to consider it.

After a few weeks, I decided that the fairest thing to do about the tickets was to post James's ticket back to him. After all, he had paid for it. I did that, and I brought my own ticket back to Ticketmaster to get my money back. As it turned out, Elton John had to cancel his concert because he was sick, so it was just as well I posted James's ticket back to him.

A few days after we were back in Dublin, my best friend Clare suggested we go into town to try doing some salsa dancing. A small group of us—Clare, her twin sister Denise, Jessica and myself—went to a pub in the city centre called Turk's Head one Tuesday night, and started a ten-week course in salsa dancing for beginners. I really enjoyed it. When the ten weeks were over, we had the option of continuing on to the improvers' class. We all moved on to the improvers' class, but after a few weeks the other girls decided it wasn't for them and stopped going. But I loved it, so I continued going on my own, and started making lots of friends. Hilary was the director and the main teacher. She was lovely and friendly and a very good teacher. Phil was a lovely man who took your money when you were paying for the class. He really made me feel so at home.

After all the classes were finished, there was a salsa club. The lights were turned down and people just danced to the music with whoever they wanted to. One night at the club I met a girl called Pamela and we became good friends. She had been dancing for quite some time and was a lot better at it than me. On Saturday nights, Hilary gave workshops where you could get more practice, and help on improving your dancing. I enjoyed meeting more new people here as well.

Chapter 37

On New Year's Eve 2009, I went out with some friends to a pub in Rathmines. We had an amazing night. At first we were downstairs having our drinks and taking photographs, but after a while we moved upstairs. I wasn't dressed very appropriately for going out. I was wearing jeans and boots and I was getting far too hot. As we were mingling I was introduced to a lovely man whose name was Daniel. We got on well. As the night went on I was just getting hotter and hotter. I said to one of the girls I'd come with that I felt like taking off my boots and my socks. She said, "why not". I knew that this was something I shouldn't really do, but I was so uncomfortably hot that I had to. It was one of the best things I ever did.

After a few minutes I felt uncomfortable standing on the floor in my bare feet. I was a bit worried that I'd stand on some broken glass and I felt it was a bit dangerous. So I decided to stand up on one of the small stools. I was standing there for just a minute or two and then out of the blue a man's hand appeared in front of me. I took his hand and he guided me up on to the table in front of me. They were playing great music on that particular night, lots of eighties music, so this was my opportunity to dance on the table in front of everybody.

Immediately I started dancing on the table. There were loads of men and women standing around the table singing to the music as well. After a few minutes my friends started to get up on the table as well. I thought to myself (Oh no, look what I've done). The table was beginning to wobble. I felt safe there by myself as I was sober, but my friends were drunk so I got a bit worried. I decided to step down onto a stool beside the table. One of the men suddenly started shaking my hand and said, "Fair play, fair play". I had livened up the pub big time. It was a great New Year's Eve.

A little while later, a bouncer came around and told me to put on my shoes. I was in no hurry to put my boots back on as I knew I'd just get too hot again. A few minutes later a man wanted me to get up on the table and start dancing again. I said,

"But I'll get in trouble".

He said, "I'll help you down really fast if you see him, you're my party girl".

So I got up on the table again and started dancing. I was in my element. Then I saw the bouncer again so I jumped down into the man's arms. Soon after that one of my friends persuaded me to put my boots back on.

A little while after that a man who was quite drunk started coming on to me. His two pathetic chat up lines were, "That brace is very sexy" and "I think you'd be very interesting". Then he started to get me to walk backwards towards the door, which led to a stairs and a way outside. As I was coming to the door he nipped me on the cheek. I said, "Don't bite me".

A few minutes later when we were standing on the top of the stairs he nipped me on the other cheek. I said,

"I told you not to bite me".

Then I walked back into the pub and he followed me back in. I suggested we swap mobile numbers but he wasn't interested. It looked to me like he just had one thing on his mind. He started putting his arms around me. I tried to stop him saying,

"Let's just dance".

He wasn't interested in dancing. I started getting a bit nervous and was looking around for my friends but couldn't see any of them. Next thing Daniel turned up beside us. He said to me,

"You want to dance?" and took me away from him.

Soon it was time for us to leave, but before we left I went up to Daniel. I told him he was the man of the night for me and gave him a kiss on the cheek. When we went outside the ground was covered in snow about one inch deep. There were no taxis and there was hardly anyone around. We went over to the taxi rank and while we were there a young man came up to us. He wanted to use my mobile phone to contact his girlfriend, as his had run out of power. I gave him my mobile and he was very grateful. I told him I trusted him and he said,

"I trust you too".

As he was trying to phone his girlfriend she turned up in her car right beside us. In return for letting him use my phone they gave us a lift home. We were very lucky as there was hardly any chance of us getting a taxi that night. I told my friend that I felt my dad was looking out for us that night.

One night in February, Pamela asked me if I wanted to come out with a group of people from salsa. They were going out to celebrate one of the guy's birthdays and I told her I'd love to. We went to a lovely Moroccan restaurant and afterwards we went to the Market Bar which I'd never been to before, and I didn't take to it at all.

After some time had passed, I realised that that was where we were going to be for the rest of the night, so I started mingling in the crowd talking to men. One of the men mentioned that he was in the media business. This seemed similar enough to what I had done in the past so I latched on to him. I found out that his name was Alex and I talked with him and another lady for most of the night. At one stage Alex went off and brought back three stools. I asked him where he was from and he told me "Fermanagh". I talked quite a bit about James as it had only been a few months since we broke up. I think I said quite a lot of bad stuff about James but then the woman said to me,

"But you went out with this man for five years".

So then I described him and said quite a few good things about him. I said "kind, loving, caring, gentle, so gentle, and he really took care of me".

Alex said that he'd been in a long relationship but it had broken up. When he told us that he'd been living in Dublin for about twenty years I got curious about his age. So I said to him,

"What age were you when you left Fermanagh?"

Alex paused for a bit and then said,

"Well, I'm forty . . . now".

I couldn't believe it. He only looked about thirty five. I thought to myself, he's ten years older than me so there's not really any chance of us being together. Then I said to him,

"What was it like growing up in Fermanagh?"

Alex described it to me and at the end he said, "learned to kiss".

I replied, "I did that in Wexford".

We also talked about my mother, and I told Alex that she had just been diagnosed with cancer.

I was very disappointed when I saw Alex stand up to put on his jacket. I went over to him and said, "It was lovely to meet you".

He told me, "It's always good to meet a film buff".

That's me—I'm a real film buff. We'd spent a good bit of the time that night talking about films, and in particular "Avatar". Just before Alex left he said to me,

"I hope you meet a nice man".

This touched my heart. I thought it was so sweet and so selfless. I thought to myself, but I've just met a nice man. Then I put it behind me and went mingling again.

Chapter 38

April 1st was the Easter salsa party. It was a fancy dress party with the theme of "Alice in Wonderland", which had been released in the cinema about the same time. I was dressed up as the white queen. When I arrived at the party I was a bit self-conscious and cold in my costume, as I'd never gone out with friends without my legs covered before. I was moving around at the end of the dance floor trying to keep warm. I turned around and who did I see in front of me changing his shoes but Alex. I couldn't believe it. I'd thought I was never going to see him again. I was filled with joy just to be in his presence again.

Just after I saw him I said "Hey!!" Alex looked up at me then I said,

"Have you done much media?"

Alex said, "How long has it been since we saw each other last?"

I said, "About a month".

Alex said, "How's your mum?"

I said, "She's doing ok thanks".

I actually couldn't believe he'd remembered she wasn't well. Then for some reason I said, "I'm terrified I'm going to call some man by the wrong name. There are so many names, I keep forgetting".

Then I said, "But I do remember yours".

I bent over and whispered into his right ear, "Alex".

He couldn't remember mine and said, "That's what you get for being old".

I told him "Sarah".

Just before I left to go to the salsa class Alex said to me, "We'll have a dance later".

I nodded. I hadn't planned to dance with him at all but I was delighted that he'd brought it up. As I was talking to him I was so happy and relaxed that it felt like I wasn't wearing anything.

Later on that night there was a dancing egg and spoon competition. When I heard Hilary asking people to take part I immediately got up. I had got into the habit of getting up just to make other people get up, even if I hadn't much chance of winning. After a good crowd of people got up the competition started. The way it worked was that you had to balance a Cadbury's cream egg on a small plastic spoon and dance at the same time. I was pretty bad at this, I even found it difficult to just balance the egg never mind dance as well. If I'm nervous, my hand shakes quite a bit and I think that's got something to do with my medication. I dropped my egg and ended up being the second person out.

When I was sitting down on the floor, at the front of the crowd of people watching the competition, I noticed Alex. Alex was doing very well, he had the egg perfectly balanced and was dancing away without a bother. At one stage I cheered him on. I shouted out "GO Al". Alex and another man came joint first, so Alex got a prize of an Easter egg. After all the games and performances were over, the lights went off and the dance floor got packed full of dancers again. I saw Alex chatting to someone and I approached him from behind, put my hand on his shoulder and said, "Well done". Alex glanced around saying "Thanks", and continued talking. Then I went to get some water.

Sometime after that Alex came over to me, took my hand and walked with me onto the dance floor, and we had our first dance. I really enjoyed it and as we were dancing I was noticing his shirt and I said to him,

"Was that the shirt you wore the last day?"

He said he didn't know and that he had loads of shirts. I loved the feel of his shirt. It was a red, silk shirt with black dots.

I told him, "You were great with the egg".

Alex replied, "Well, it's what I do".

I said to him, "Are you going to be the man to get this skirt over my hips?" The skirt was too big for me.

Alex just said, "You can hoist it up if you want".

I told him, "I don't think it will, it just feels like it will".

When the song was over Alex said, "Thank you". I thanked him in return and then we went our separate ways.

That night, when I got home I went on to "Facebook" and looked for Alex to add him as a friend. I found him and I sent him a friend request. Then I decided to send him a message in case he didn't know who I was. In the message I thanked him for the dance and said that I hoped we'd bump into each other again sometime soon. I also mentioned how happy I was to be back in my jeans again and that the white skirt was making me so nervous. I was waiting for him to accept me as a friend for about a week and I thought to myself maybe he thinks I'm too young, as he was forty and I was a very young thirty one. I was beginning to give up on him.

The following Thursday I was sitting on a stool in the Garda club when Alex showed up in front of me, waving at me. My jaw dropped and I didn't breathe for about seven seconds. I had said in my message that I hoped we'd bump into each other soon, but I definitely hadn't expected to see him this soon. I got off my stool and went over to him and his friend and I told him this. His friend said, "Oh he's always here", which I knew wasn't true because I'd been there every Thursday since the start of the year and I'd only seen Alex there once before. Alex said that they were going over to the other side of the room. I said "Okay" and went back to sit on my stool.

Then I noticed Alex standing by the post near me by himself so I went over to him. We chatted for a bit and then I asked him,

"So why didn't you accept me as a friend on Facebook?"

Alex replied, "Oh, I prefer to keep Facebook just for family and friends abroad, no offence".

I shook my head and said, "It's ridiculous anyway having all these friends that you're never in touch with".

Alex said, "That's exactly what I mean".

Then I said to him, "So, are you a salsa teacher?"

Alex replied, "I used to be a salsa teacher".

Then I told him I'd gone to see Alice in Wonderland in the cinema and that I love Johnny Depp.

Alex said, "He's a good actor".

Then I told him that my favourite film is, '*Pirates of the Caribbean: The Curse of the Black Pearl*' and he said, "I must watch that".

Then Alex said we'd have a dance later and left me.

I went back to my stool. I had some lousy men ask me to dance that night and had a man that was quite drunk coming on to me as well, so in that sense it was a pretty poor night. Later on in the night towards the end of the club, I was beginning to think that maybe Alex had decided not to dance with me. Then a foreign man brought me onto the dance floor into a ring of couples. I'd watched people doing this particular dance before but I'd never done it myself. I was quite reluctant to do it but I managed okay in the end. Then I went back to my stool.

Next thing a voice comes from behind me, "Hiya". It was Alex, and he'd saved the last dance for me. This was a lovely, sweet surprise for me as I'd kind of given up on my dance with him at this stage of the night.

Alex said to me, "Do you want to dance?" Then he took my hand and brought me out onto the dance floor. While we were dancing Alex asked me what the dance was that I'd just been doing.

I replied, "I don't know, I was kind of dragged into it".

Then I asked him, "How was your Easter?"

He said, "Good, I went home, how was yours?"

I said, "My aunt died".

Alex said, "Sorry".

I told him that she'd had cancer for years. At one stage I said to Alex, "I love this move".

It was the crucifix move. After I said that to him he did an unusual move with his arms, a move I'd never seen before and I said "Cool". When the song was over the lights came on and we thanked each other. As we were walking off the dance floor another man just came along and gave me a dance. Alex went over to sit on a stool and watched me dance with this man. When the dance was over I went to head home. I looked over at Alex and said to him, "Well, I'll see you around" and left. Alex waved at me as I left the room. When I got home I was thinking to myself, I think I've found my man, and was really on quite a high. I was in love with Alex but I didn't know if he felt anything for me.

Chapter 39

One Tuesday night at Turk's Head after the salsa class I went over to Martin, the salsa teacher and told him that I'd never been thrown around the dance floor so much in my life. He took me over to the side and started talking to me about how the class had gone, and I told him it was okay. He took me aside and showed me how to move my ribs from side to side which I found quite difficult, as I couldn't sense my body as easily as others due to my epilepsy. While he was showing me he said, "Because you have a fabulous rib cage". I mastered it after a few minutes. Then he showed me how to do the steps 1,3,5,7, left, right, left, right. The compliment went over my head and that night when I got home I sent a message to Alex:

Hi Alex,

They played my favourite song at salsa tonight Kilo (I think). I love it. I don't understand the words because it's in Spanish but by the feel of it I'd say it's quite an emotional song. It's quite a slow song so they don't play it at the club and they normally don't play it at intermediate either but they did tonight. It was okay at the start of the session because I could lead myself but as the moves got more complicated it was quite disappointing not being able to dance to my favourite song as all the men were off beat. Anyway, I'm sure they'll play it again another night and I'll be able to let myself go and dance to my favourite song. Okay handsome, I'll let you go and if you decide to turn up in the Garda club to give me a dance could you wear your silky shirt. I love the feel of the silk on you. Take care of yourself. Love Sarah.

The next morning when I woke, all that was going around in my mind was the rib cage compliment. For the next week I was debating with myself and I was kind of up in a knot about whether I should say something to Martin or not. I really loved Alex—he was the man I wanted to be with but was that going to happen? In the end, I felt that maybe I should keep my options open. I felt that Martin's compliment was so unique, so specific, and so masculine that I had to return the compliment. I also wondered why he was complimenting me, and was thinking, does he compliment all of the girls he teaches or am I special?

After the Tuesday salsa class the following week I went over to Martin and thanked him for his compliment. I told him that I get a lot of compliments and that his was unique. Then I gave him a pathetic compliment in return. We had a brief chat, I asked him where he was from and he said "Limerick".

I said, "I thought you were a country man".

He said "Yea, I'm a culchie". He asked me for my name and then he left to go home. I stayed in the club for a bit and then headed home myself.

The next week I didn't enjoy the salsa class at all. I talked to Martin briefly afterwards about one of the men grabbing on to my tummy and he said,

"Well I tried to tell them not to."

I left the club quite early that night and as I was leaving I looked into Martin's eyes as I passed by him. I'd been feeling pretty bad about the compliment I'd given him, and felt I really needed to find a better one, one that would be able to compete with his rib cage compliment. As Martin was such a handsome man I felt there had to be a compliment I could think of. As I was walking to the bus stop I decided that I'd found the perfect compliment . . . His eyes, Martin has fabulous eyes. When I was looking in his eyes as I was leaving

I saw a very concerned, 'what did I do wrong' kind of expression coming from them which was pretty impressive.

Two days after that, when I was at salsa in the Garda club, Martin turned up selling tickets for "Concern". I went to buy some tickets from him, he thanked me and I said to him,

"How could I not with you selling them".

Martin took the money and went to get me my change. When he came back, I said to him,

"Do you know, you have lovely eyes, did anyone ever tell you that?"

Martin said "thanks".

Then he said to me, "That's as good as the rib cage compliment". I was very satisfied with that and left him saying "Tuesday" as I walked away. When Martin was going around collecting the tickets at his salsa class the following Tuesday, he stopped in front of me and gave me a deep look into my eyes. A smile began to emerge on my face.

The following week after the salsa class I went over to Martin and asked him which way he was heading home. He said "Georges street" and I said I'd walk with him a bit of the way. As we walked out of the pub together he opened the door for me and I said "Such a gentleman". I was a bit uptight because I'd worn a dress to salsa for the first time. As we walked down the street I said under my breath,

"One of the men gave out to me".

Martin reacted to this in a very inappropriate way. He turned to face me in an instant and in an almost scarily protective way he said, "Who gave out to YOU?"

This was exactly the same way that my dad, God rest his soul, had reacted when I arrived home from the nightclub with black circles all over my neck. My dad had said "Who did that to YOU?"

I loved that memory so much, my dad's protective attitude towards anyone daring to treat his precious daughter's beautiful body like that. Now Martin had robbed this memory from me and when I found out that he had a girlfriend I was so upset that I had a seizure in bed one morning afterwards.

This seizure was different from the other seizures I'd had over the past number of years. This time I was agitated for about half an hour after the seizure. What was actually happening was that I was straining my memory to try and remember how things had gone between Martin and myself. When I was conscious again, I was surrounded for the rest of the day by the dark aura I'd gone through for years before and which I thought I was past at this stage. I was lying on the couch feeling miserable and I was nearly crying as I looked over to my dad's empty chair and remembered that the last time I was feeling like this my dad was sitting in that chair keeping me company. Now my dad was gone and my lovely memory of him was gone too. I was feeling awful, but then the picture of Alex turning up in front of me and waving at me that night came into my mind. My dad wasn't there for me anymore but Alex was. I decided that I should message Alex and let him know how he had helped me through this hard day.

In the message I described the aura to him, which I'd never been able to describe to anyone before. I thanked him for helping me through a really hard day and said that I hoped we'd see each other really soon. That evening when I checked my hotmail I saw that I'd received a message from Alex, which I hadn't expected at all:

Hi Sarah,

Thank you for your nice message.

I hope all is going better now.

See you at salsa soon.

Alex.

Chapter 40

The next Thursday was the summer party in the Garda club. At one stage during the evening I caught Alex's eyes and he came over to me. He was concerned about how I was. I told him I was grand and that I was looking forward to going to Maynooth for a weekend of dancing. I asked him if he was going and he said he wasn't. We left it at that and went mingling. Alex didn't dance with me at all that night.

At the end of the night I went up to Alex as we were all leaving the room and I asked him if he wanted to set a proper date. Alex said,

"NO, I'm pursuing something else now but thank you".

I said, "Not a bother, I'll just cross you off the list, but you'll at least give me a dance next time?"

Alex said, "Grab me".

We chatted a bit and I mentioned that he hadn't been in the Garda club for two months. Alex said, "Have you been here every Thursday?"

I said, "Yes, but not last Thursday".

Alex said, "I wasn't here last Thursday".

I said "I didn't think you were".

I told him that I also did salsa in Turk's Head on Tuesdays. Then as we parted I looked at Alex and said, "A dance next time then", and we left it at that. I didn't know when I was going to see him again.

The following Thursday I had an amazing night at the Garda club. Alex was there again. I spent a lot of time going around the room asking men to dance. There were so many men there that I knew that night, but Alex was the icing on the cake. After I'd danced with all the men I went and stood in front of Alex. I'd say I was actually looking my very best that night. I was dressed in my perfect little black dress, with bare shoulders and bare legs, a silver necklace and silver shoes. I had my hair down and I had no weight on me because of all the dancing.

I said to Alex, "This is the first time you've been here two weeks in a row".

Alex replied, "I haven't been here for three months".

Then I bent down and looked into his eyes and said to him, "That's what I mean".

He jumped off his chair, took my hand and said, "Let's dance", and he brought me onto the dance floor. It was an amazing dance. I told him all about my trip to Maynooth. Alex did some amazing dance moves with me that night. One of them I remember very clearly was when he swung me backwards into his arms and then back up again. When the song ended Alex said, "Thank you very much", and I thanked him in return.

One night pretty soon afterwards I sent Alex another message. I told him about how I thought that night was amazing and that it was even better than the New Year's Eve night when I was dancing on the table, and that I'd thought that night would never be topped. I also told him not to stay away too long.

I'd been looking at Alex's profile on Facebook quite regularly as I loved looking at the photographs he had on it. One day I was looking at his profile and I noticed a quote he'd put up. It was a Bob Marley quote—*The truth is, everyone is going to hurt you, you've just got to find the ones worth suffering for.* This quote had quite an effect on me and I was pretty upset by it. I was feeling for Alex, "You suffer, I suffer". I also felt that that meant I was going to hurt him and I couldn't bare the idea of hurting Alex. For the next few days that was all I could think about. Alex and the quote were deep inside me and I felt more in love with him than ever.

I felt I had to message Alex again and for some reason I remembered a Christmas card that my dad had given to my mother years before. My Dad had ended his Christmas message "All my love". This was the way I was feeling about Alex at this time. I was totally in love with him and could feel nothing else. So I sent Alex a message showing my pain and really pinning it on him. I also thanked him for the joy and happiness he had filled my heart with and told him that nobody had ever made me as happy as he did. I said that I only wished '*I could make you as happy as you make me*' and ended it "All my love".

A few days later when I checked his profile there was a horrible photograph up there. It was the kind of photo that nobody in their right mind would put up as a profile picture. He was looking so depressed, he was dressed horribly and looked like he didn't want to live his life. I could hardly look at this photograph of him, and the message it portrayed to me was '*I don't deserve you*'. I left the computer thinking, okay that's the end of that.

Later that night I was remembering how miserable he looked in the photo and felt that I could at least try and cheer him up, give him a reason to live, even if it wasn't going to be more than that and I thought to myself, '*do the Lord's work*', which was something I got from James. James was so religious and he was always going on about "doing the Lord's work".

I sent a message to Alex. I told him why I loved dancing with HIM, that I felt safe on the dance floor, that I knew nobody was going to step on my feet or bang into me and bruise me. I told him that when we were dancing the last time it felt like there was nobody else in the room but the two of us. I told him that I thought this was amazing and kind of special, that it showed how happy and relaxed I was. I also told him how he had touched my heart over the number of times we'd been together. I asked him if he wanted to share any of his pain with me but also said that he didn't have to, and told him I'd be in touch the next night. I was thinking about the man in the photograph and how miserable he looked and that he needed my support.

The next morning I got a message from Alex, thanking me for my messages and saying that he'd prefer if we kept our communication to when we were on the dance floor. He ended the message, "I do hope you understand".

I felt this was fair enough and replied:

> *If that's what you want Alex that's fine with me, but please reassure me that you're alright. That photo of you is terrifying me, I'm in bits over it, why did you have to put it on Facebook? It's killing me.*

I was tied up in knots all that day. The photo was going around and around in my head. I felt like they were two different people. The Alex I knew looked between thirty five and forty. This photo made him look between forty five and fifty. That night I went to Facebook and I dragged out all five photos of Alex on to my desktop—the four photos of Alex that I had enjoyed looking at over the past few months, and the weird one of him that he'd just put up the other day. Only one of the four photos had facial expression coming from it and it was taken from a distance. I also got the feeling that it was taken a good many years ago. Two of the other photos were portrait photos and the other was a pose from quite a distance. The weird photo was the full face and full of miserable expression. I compared each of the four to the new one many times. I noticed the face slightly broader in the new one but didn't think much of it. The way the hair was styled was quite different but not enough to think that he hadn't styled it that way. Then I looked at my favourite photo of Alex, his portrait photo, the one he had up as his main photo on Facebook. As I looked at it I noticed that when I looked at his lips I felt that deep love inside me. Then I looked at the lips of the man in the weird photo and I couldn't bear the idea of kissing them. This convinced me that it wasn't the same man. I had felt during the day that it was like they were two different men and now I was pretty sure they were. I was quite happy and reassured that night as I went to bed.

The next morning I got a message from Alex saying *"I'm fine thanks"*. I decided to return his message and I apologised for going overboard about the photograph. I told him that I'd been studying the photographs and said that after some time it dawned on me that it wasn't the same man. I told him that it was the lips that did it, that his lips were ten times more kissable than the other man's. Then after sending that message I looked at the photos again and I saw an amazing resemblance at the side of the mouth in one of the four photos of Alex. I decided to send him another message and I told him I wasn't so sure and that I hoped I hadn't offended him. I told him that it just didn't make sense. How was I in love with this man and how did I dance with him the way I did just a few weeks ago? I told him I just couldn't understand it.

A few days later I became psychotic. It was a different type of psychosis than before. This time I hadn't had a seizure and my mind was clearer. It was more involved with how I was feeling than what I was thinking. This time, throughout the psychosis, Alex was involved in one way or another. It also lasted longer than usual. About the second or third night into the psychosis I started to message Alex telling him how I was feeling and how scared I was. I was pregnant again, only this time I was pregnant with a miracle baby that had been conceived while Alex and myself were dancing. I told Alex this in a message and I also told him that when I was reaching puberty I decided that I just wanted to love one man for the rest of my life. I told him he was that man and that he gave me everything I needed—joy and happiness, without wanting anything in return—and that that made him very special. When I came back to normality again I messaged him:

> *I'm so sorry Alex I was psychotic. My feelings get mixed up sometimes and since I last saw my doctor I've been affected by men. I'll tell you something Alex, this has been the most enjoyable psychotic episode I've gone through, and looking at these mixed-up feelings, you can surely see just how much I love you. Take care. Sarah.*

The next Thursday when I was in the Garda club I was thinking to myself is he going to turn up. When I saw him, dressed in his silk shirt, I thought to myself 'Oh my God he's here'. We made definite eye contact that night but that was about it. It just so happened, that that night loads of men came up to me asking me to dance. I was getting up and down off my stool and Alex was just standing by the post in his silk shirt watching me. I never asked one man to dance with me that night. Then at one stage while I was sitting on my stool Alex walked straight past me and he looked pretty annoyed. It's gas, one thing that really struck me as he was walking past me was his shoes. I loved his shoes. I just continued sitting on the stool for the rest of the night thinking that he might come back and ask me to dance but he didn't.

Five days later on Tuesday in Turk's Head I was dancing with a man in the intermediate class. It was near the end of the class and while I was dancing I saw Alex out of the corner of my eye. I wasn't certain so I took my eyes off the man I was dancing with and focused totally away to the side. It *was* Alex and he was standing at the top of the steps looking down at me. I thought to myself, 'Wow, what's he doing here?' I'd been coming to Turk's Head to do salsa on Tuesdays for nearly a year now, and never once had I seen Alex there. As soon as the class was over, I went straight over to him and I said, "What are you doing here, I don't mean you shouldn't be here but you're never here".

He said, "Oh, I was just passing and I thought I'd drop in".

I said, "Stop looking at me like that, you're making me nervous looking at me like that".

He said, "Well go and dance, that's what you came here to do".

I said, "Do you want to dance?"

He said "NO".

Then he said, "I don't know what to say Sarah, I don't know what to say".

I put my hand on his shoulder and said, "Well, just talk, you said I don't know enough".

Alex butted in, "I don't want to share my life story with you".

I said, "That's okay".

Then he said, "I don't want my life any more complicated than it already is".

I said, "Okay, is your life complicated?"

He didn't say anything else. I walked down the steps, turned around and looking him in the eyes said, "Well, you'll at least give me a dance sometime".

Alex didn't say anything to that, he just looked a bit taken aback and maybe gave a nod. I went back to the other men and danced for a bit. When I was leaving with Stephen, one of the men in the salsa class that I'd got a lift from a few times previously, I saw Alex dancing bachata with another woman and I was wishing I was dancing with him.

Two days later Alex turned up in the Garda club again. When I saw him I decided I should approach him. I walked up to him and I slid my two fingers across his back a bit. He turned around and I told him how I was feeling.

I said, "My heart is full of joy".

Alex said, "Relax".

I said, "Thanks", and then he told me to jump in and join in the dancing. I didn't. Alex said he was going to get some water.

Then he said "I'll see YOU later". As he left he put two of his fingers on my hip and checked out my figure.

I said "Okay Alex".

For the rest of the night I sat on a stool and Alex sat on his stool up the room a bit. A few men asked me to dance but nothing like the first night when Alex showed up in his silk shirt. Towards the end of the night, Alex got up, got a lady and danced the bachata with moves that I'd never seen before. He was such an amazing dancer. I thought to myself '*I love him so much*'. In the past when Alex danced to bachata it was mostly the closed position, hip to hip, and when I looked at him I loved the way that I could see how he was feeling the music and how he was moving to the music.

Alex had done hardly any of that kind of dancing since I'd told him how I felt, which I thought was kind of strange. There was one thing about Alex tonight that I thought was quite odd. It was his shoes. The shoes he was wearing were so not him. Alex would normally wear classy gentleman's shoes—the kind you'd wear with trousers or a suit, shoes that wouldn't suit jeans at all. Tonight he was wearing quite casual black shoes with metal on them, shoes that would only go with jeans—they wouldn't suit trousers at all. At the end of the night when the lights came on I decided to approach Alex. I went up to him and said, "Did you forget to ask me to dance?"

Alex misheard me and replied, "I didn't ask you to dance".

I replied, "No, I said did you forget to ask me to dance".

He said, "I did, but don't worry we'll have a dance again sometime".

Then we said goodnight to each other and I walked out of the room.

The following Thursday was my birthday night. This was a great night and even though it was my thirty-second birthday it felt like my twenty-first. As soon as I arrived at the Garda club I started to ask people how old they thought I was. Hilary thought I was twenty-five. Another one of the men thought I was twenty-two, another one twenty-three. When I saw Alex that night, the first thing I noticed that was weird about him was his hair. It was styled the very same way as the man in the strange photograph. His clothes were very unusual as well, and the only thing that made sense to me about Alex that night was the shoes. He was wearing the same strange shoes as the previous night. I also didn't feel any connection with this man, my heart couldn't care less whether he was watching me or not. This man also had a very different style of dance. He didn't impress me at all.

After quite some time when I was finishing dancing with one man, this man who I'd never be able to call Alex, because I felt I didn't know him, caught my attention by waving at me. Now Alex had waved at me before and it was nothing like that. I went to get some water and then decided I should approach him and maybe try and make some physical contact. When I went over to him he asked me if I was having fun. I shrugged my shoulders and said "Yes". I asked him how his week was. He said it was fine, nothing bad. Then I rubbed his back.

Before I had approached him, he'd been talking to some man. Then the first really strange thing that happened was that he suddenly got up and moved down the room a bit. This wasn't like Alex at all. I felt it was quite rude, and I wouldn't consider Alex to be rude. After he moved I got up and decided to approach him again. I went up to him and started the conversation by asking him why he decided to put up the quote on Facebook. Then something else weird happened.

He said, "What quote?"

I thought this was strange because it was the only quote he had up on his profile page. I told him the quote and he just said, "Well, I just thought it was a good quote and I also think it's true".

I replied "NO, that's the most painful thing I've ever read".

Then I started talking about my birthday and I asked him what age he thought I was and he replied, "I don't know your age".

I thought that was odd too, because I'd said in one of my messages to Alex that my dad had died three and a half years ago when I was twenty-eight.

I said to him, "Thirty two, it's nice to look young but when people start treating you young . . ."

Then I mentioned to him, "I wonder when I'm going to get my ring of men".

When it's someone's birthday at salsa, they put on special birthday music and you're called into the centre of the dance floor. Then the men make a circle around you and take turns dancing with you.

When I said this he said to me, "Go up and tell the DJ".

I said "I told Hilary" and he said, "There's a new DJ now".

I went up to the DJ and I told him that it was my birthday and then went back to one of the other women. A few minutes later the DJ came down to me and said,

"You didn't tell me your name".

I told him "Sarah".

He said, "And what age are you, twenty one?"

I laughed and said, "That's the youngest I've got so far".

He said, "We'll leave it then".

He went back to the stage and a few minutes later he announced to the crowd,

"I hear there's a birthday girl here tonight, Sarah, and she's twenty one".

I ran up to him and told him I was thirty-two. He said, "Actually she's thirty two". Everyone laughed and then he said, "Well, she's honest".

The music started and I was standing in the middle of the dance floor by myself. Then one man ran over to me and started dancing with me. The DJ said,

"Any other men who want to can come onto the floor as well".

I was told afterwards that there were about ten men in the circle around me.

After I'd recovered from that I approached the man who I presumed must be Alex's brother again. As I was walking up to him, the lady he was talking to wished me a happy birthday and I said "thanks". Then I said to Alex's brother,

"Thank you for telling me to go up to the DJ". He turned to face me, and that was the first time we really made proper eye contact. When I saw his eyes something didn't seem right. They didn't have the same eyes.

Anyway, I said to him, "Well, are you going to give me a birthday dance?"

He nodded, and then I asked him if he was going to come and get me.

He said, "I'll come and get you, I'll just finish up here first".

I left and went over to another woman for a chat. A few minutes later he came over to me, took my hand and brought me onto the dance floor. While we were dancing I started to talk about the quote again.

He said, "Can we not talk about it anymore?"

I said, "Deal".

A few minutes later I said to him, "Blame the quote, I wouldn't have opened my heart to you if it wasn't for the quote".

He replied, "Don't worry about it".

At the end of the song he looked me straight in the eyes and said, "Happy Birthday".

I gave him a big smile and said, "Thank you".

Then he left the Garda club. I was so happy. Even though I was pretty sure it wasn't Alex who had wished me a happy birthday it still felt the same.

It was around this time that I got very sick. I don't know what happened exactly, it's a big blur. I woke up in hospital without any idea of how I'd got there. I'd had seizures because, for some unknown reason, I came off my medication. I was very thin as well, and I don't know how long I'd been off my food before my brother, Peter found me. I was actually having great fun in hospital. I was having loads of visitors. Some of my aunts and uncles and even some of my cousins came in to see me. Friends of mine came in as well and the parish priest came, which was a big surprise.

All the time I was in Tallaght hospital, and especially when I was on my own, I was thinking of Alex. In particular, I was remembering the Easter party when I turned around and he was in front of me. I'd thought I was never going to see him again. I was remembering the way I'd reacted and I could feel the joy in my heart when I went "Hey" to myself, which was what I'd said to Alex the moment I saw him. I was in Tallaght hospital for about two weeks and then without really telling me, they sent me off to St. Edmundsbury, a hospital where people who have mental difficulties go.

I had my own private room in the hospital which was great, but I didn't like it there at all. While I was there, I only mixed with the other patients when I was going down to eat at meal times. I didn't go to any of the classes or activities that were going on, I just kept to myself. The grounds were beautiful and the weather was glorious so I used to go outside with my mobile phone and listen to the radio and walk for miles. I'd say I walked about ten miles a day. I used to dance by myself outside as well.

Alex was still on my mind the whole time. One day Pamela, a girl I'd met through salsa came in to see me. I think she'd heard there was a pool table there, so she came in to play pool with me. I started talking to her about Alex. Pamela knew a very close friend of Alex's whose name was Joanna. Then one day, off her own bat, Pamela went to Joanna and asked her what the chances were of Alex and myself hooking up. While I was lying on my bed one day, I got a text from Pamela. It said that she'd spoken to Joanna about Alex and myself hooking up and that Joanna had said he was in a relationship with someone else. I thought to myself God love this someone else, whoever it is surely deserves to have a name. I'll tell you something though, I never believed that Alex was in a relationship with someone else. I believe that if he was he would have told me. I mean what was Joanna supposed to say anyway? I was the one who didn't really want to hook up with him. At first I was actually quite mad at Joanna, but now I'm really annoyed with Pamela for going off without asking me first.

One day I had a visit from my cousin Anna and over about an hour I told her all about Alex and how we'd met. When I'd finished, Anna said to me,

"Sarah, that's quite a romantic story, maybe if you tell the doctors they'd be able to help you".

I never told anybody else the story. Sure it takes about an hour to tell anyway. While I was there I was given a sheet of paper where I had to write down what I wanted to get out of my stay in St. Edmundsbury. I put down that I wanted to go home and I wanted to go on the pill with confidence.

Over time, I was put on the pill and I was allowed to go home. A few of my friends were saying to me that you should only be on the pill if you're in a sexual relationship and that there can be very bad side effects. After a while, and after a couple of weeks back at salsa with no sign of Alex, I was beginning to feel stupid. I said to my brother,

"Do you think I'm mad going on the pill?"

Peter said, "Well, sure at least you'll know how it affects you".

So I stayed on the pill for the whole month even though there was no sign of Alex. I think the main reason I got sick and went on the pill was because I was scared. I'd always had this thing that because I was a virgin there was no chance of me getting pregnant, and when Alex suddenly gave the impression that my virginity was going to disappear for ever I felt I was losing something and the chance of getting pregnant was huge. I'd been a virgin for so long that the idea of losing my virginity, and losing it to someone I didn't know all that well, was huge and I was quite anxious about it.

Around the end of October or the beginning of November you could say I was kind of over Alex, but then he turned up in the Garda club again. This time Alex's image was totally different but I don't want to go into that too much. When I first saw him that night, for some unknown reason, I felt like I was being stabbed in my heart, just briefly though. Later in the night I saw Alex leaving the room with a girl with long blonde hair with his hand on her back. At this stage I was really feeling, *'well, that's the end of that',* and I was ready to move on to another man in the salsa club. Then towards the end of the night Alex approached me.

He said, "Sarah".

I replied to him in a very formal manner, "Hello Alex, how are you?"

Alex didn't answer me. Instead he said, "You got your brace off, it looks well".

I lowered my head, with my eyes still glued to him. I gave him a big smile and said, "Thanks, it's great to have it off".

He said, "I'm sure it is, I'm going to head now, I'll talk to you next time".

I said, "Okay, take care".

When I got home, I was thinking to myself *'Shit what's going on? It's still not over'*. After I came out of hospital, I'd been talking to my brother about the situation of Alex and myself, and I told him that I'd given myself to Alex while I was psychotic. I told Peter what Alex had said to me. Peter said,

"Well, it's his problem, you tried. If he wants you he'll get you".

I think I mentioned something about it being over and Peter said to me, "It's not over".

I'd been going on about Alex to Pamela quite a bit and I think it was getting on her nerves because she said to me,

"Can you not take it that he doesn't want you?"

This remark hurt me a bit but what I replied was, "It doesn't matter whether he wants me or not, it's a very deep love".

She said, "Are you not over him?"

I said, "Not since he complimented me".

Pamela didn't have a reply to that.

On St. Patrick's Day there was a special salsa flag party in the Garda club. Everyone had to dress up in the colours of their national flag. It was a good night, and there were some great performances, one from a group of ballet dancers and another from Bachata Ireland, but Alex wasn't there.

Towards the end of the night, someone stood on my foot and dug their heel into it. I was in so much pain that I decided I'd go home. As I was walking out of the Garda club there were some foreign men leaving at the same time. I was probably complaining about my foot and when I got to the edge of the footpath to get a taxi home, one of them came up to me and asked, "Where are you going?"

I said, "Home".

He said, "You're going home at this time on Paddy's Day?"

It was about half eleven or twelve.

He said, "You look like a lovely girl. What's your name?"

I said "Sarah" and he said his name was Sam.

He said, "Come for a drink with us".

I said, "I can't, I have a man in my heart".

Sam said to me, "Well, at least you're honest".

Then we went our separate ways.

Alex was still in my heart, but the more he stayed away from me the fainter the feeling was. All the same though, I still knew and still know now that I love Alex to bits.

I went to Mass today and I really enjoyed it. I hadn't been at Mass for weeks or even months because my body clock was, and probably still is, in a mess but last night I decided I'd try and get up at twelve and go to the half past twelve mass. When I went into the church I realised that it was Palm Sunday. What a coincidence—the day I chose to return to Mass was a special feast day.

After Mass I got the bus into town and I went to see Red Riding Hood for the second time. When I went outside afterwards, the weather was glorious. The sun was shining and the sky was lovely and blue, so I decided to walk home. It's a long walk, but I love walking so it doesn't seem like miles to me. As I was walking I was thinking to myself, this is my life and I love it so much. I walk, I write, I go to the cinema and I dance. Walking on a day like this makes me think, I don't need a job. I don't want to be spending time watching children. If I was playing with them that would be different, but when you're working, you spend time talking to your co-workers and that isn't my thing. I love spending time by myself and I guess that's because that's what I did growing up. I was left by myself a lot of the time and so that's who I am. Of course Alex is in my life. Alex is always with me and I'm longing for him now, which is stronger at certain times than at others.

I'm waiting for him to come back to the Garda club, and when he does, I'll go straight to him because I'm pretty sure that's what he wants. The last time Alex was in the Garda club he didn't approach me and I didn't approach him. We're really just two big flirts, so busy flirting with the opposite sex that we can't get our arms around each other. Last time he was there I saw emotion on his face, which is very unusual for Alex. I've always seen Alex as being quite reserved and to see that emotion on his face was amazing. What happened was, my favourite song came on in the club and I grabbed a man who was standing near me that I didn't know. I started to dance with him to my favourite song and I flirted with him so much—I didn't realise how much I was flirting—that got Alex really mad. That's the emotion I saw on Alex's face—madness at my flirting. That night I realised just how much he wanted me. The thing is, I gave myself, my heart to Alex over the internet so Alex couldn't really approach me. It was me who had to approach him. As far as I could tell, and judging by his body language, Alex had wanted me to go to him for months now and I felt so guilty for playing so hard to get.

Now Alex was getting back at me and I didn't blame him, but I missed him so much and I wanted him to come back to the Garda club so much. Sometimes I wondered if he'd ever come back to get me, but then I'd say to myself, *'why wouldn't he come back*?', and I didn't have an answer for that. I just reassured myself as best as I could that he would.

The Easter salsa party this year was nothing like last year, but I guess that's because Alex wasn't there. I was actually okay with the fact that Alex wasn't there, as the place was really too packed and too noisy to communicate with him the way I wanted to anyway. As the night went on I was actually getting a bit nervous that if he turned up and I couldn't go to him, or if I saw him dancing bachata, I'd be upset but neither of those things happened.

He came back!! I was sitting on a stool in the Garda club and at about 10.15 I looked over to my right and I saw Alex standing a couple of feet off the dance floor not too far from the door. He was talking to another woman, as usual. So I got off my stool and walked over to him. When I reached him he looked at me and said, "Hello".

The first thing I said to him was, "I missed you".

He didn't make any reply. Then I said to him, "We're going to be famous. I'm writing a book".

I told him the actors that had been chosen for us were Johnny Depp and Natalie Portman. Alex seemed to agree with the choice of actors. Then he said to me,

"We'll have a dance later. I'm going to dance with this woman now, we'll have a dance later".

As we parted, I slid my hand along his shoulder and then went and sat down and texted a friend to tell her that he was there. Then I asked another man to dance bachata with me. Both Alex and myself were dancing bachata with someone else and neither of us was bothered about anything, we were just enjoying the dancing. Shortly after that I saw Alex talking with another man and I decided to go over to them. When I got there, I started talking to the other man whose name I didn't get. I started to quote the introduction of my book to him and then I said to him,

"Would you buy it?"

He said, "I'd be the first in line".

I flicked my hand up and gently tapped it off Alex's chest, and without looking at him, I said,

"See, I told you we're going to be famous."

Then I told the other man, "The last line I wrote was, '*Deep down I know he'll come back*'. Then as I glided my hand softly up and down the stubble on Alex's cheek I said, "And see, here he is, he came back".

Sometime later, when Alex was walking off the dance floor I walked over to him and said, "Can I take you up on that dance now?"

We got into the dance position with my hand on his shoulder and his hand on my back. Then I said, "I'm nervous around you for some reason, this will relax me".

Alex didn't say much to me on the dance floor and I didn't ask him any questions. I did the talking on the dance floor and I told Alex that I'd ended up in hospital because of us. Alex said, "You were in hospital, why?"

I told him that I'd gone off my food and my medication. Then I told him about the doctor who was looking after me in St. Edmundsbury. I told him that this Dr. Fred Wilson had basically said to me,

"Alex is going to break your heart, Alex is in a relationship with someone else, Alex is going to take advantage of you and Alex is going to take advantage of your inheritance". Alex didn't give any reply to this. Then I looked at him and I said,

"But you didn't break my heart", to which he didn't reply either.

Alex was having great fun playing with my hips. He used to be a salsa teacher so he knew all the moves. He knew the exact count and the exact moment to tip his hand off one hip so that I'd turn and spin into his other hand, and then his other hand would tip my other hip and spin me back again. When the song was over Alex just walked off the dance floor and I followed.

Later on I said to Alex, "Do you want to replace this?"

I looked at my beautiful watch and I slid my thumb and forefinger along the sides of it. Alex said "No", and then he said to me,

"Why would I want to replace it?"

I replied, "My ex gave it to me".

Alex said to me, "Burn it, burn it", and he wasn't joking.

Just before I left the Garda club that night I went over to Alex and I gave him a kiss. I wasn't in the mood for kissing facial hair so I kissed him just at the top of his cheek, near enough to the side of his eye. Alex moved his head slightly when I kissed him as if he wasn't expecting it. Then I said to him, "I had to do that, that's for making me so happy".

Alex replied "you're welcome".

Chapter 43

Alex hasn't been at the Garda club for two months now. That doesn't bother me too much though, as I'm pretty sure he'll come back at some stage and I'm well used to waiting by now. I also love him more when I'm not with him than when I'm with him for some reason. I think that's because I'm remembering all the time we spent together and all the things he said to me and they do say that absence makes the heart grow fonder.

The thing that I do find hard is talking to women about my relationship with Alex. I hate it when they say things like, '*If he loves you why isn't he here*?' or '*You could be missing out on other opportunities*'. The other one is, '*You could have any man here*'. There are lots of men in the Garda club on a Thursday night, but I don't want just any man, I want Alex. The only thing is, the longer Alex stays away the more I think to myself, does he really want me? It's getting kind of hard loving him on a Thursday night when I'm surrounded by so many men. One lady said to me at one stage, "Tell him to hurry up and propose", so I was thinking about this and thought, maybe that's the way to go when he does come back. At least I'll know where I stand then.

I was telling another lady about this approach to Alex and she said to me,

"Sarah, you can't just go up and propose to someone you met at salsa".

I don't know, maybe I will, maybe I wont. We'll see what happens in time. Though I have to say I'm beginning to think that Alex staying away is a way of showing that he loves me, and that he's giving me time to come around to the idea of losing my virginity. I definitely wasn't ready the last time he was at the Garda club but I think I am now, and particularly if he turns up in his silk shirt. That would definitely entice me.

I've been thinking a lot about the fact that I said that Johnny Depp could play the part of Alex, and now I'm thinking that he probably wouldn't be able to pull it off. It was a friend of mine who suggested Johnny Depp anyway, without even having met Alex. Johnny Depp is a very good actor but I don't think he's like Alex at all, and it's the silk shirt and the dancing that I don't think he could pull off. I mean could you see Johnny Depp in a silk shirt doing the tango? I don't think so. I'd consider Antonio Banderas to play Alex and he's a great dancer as well.

Alex turned up at the Garda club last night. At one stage when I was standing at the edge of the dance floor watching the other dancers, I turned my head to the left and there he was. He was standing on his own with his back to the post just down the room a little bit and he was back in the image I fell in love with—the way that he was a year ago when he turned up after I told him how I felt about him. His hair was back to normal, he was in his silk shirt, black trousers and classy shoes.

I walked over to him, looked him straight in the eyes and said to him,

"Just over a year ago you told me what you didn't want. Now I'm going to tell you what I want".

I put my left hand on his shoulder and my right hand behind his neck. I slid my hand along his shirt, really enjoying the feel of the silk under my hand. Then I said to him,

"I want . . . a white gold engagement ring, and I want to NEVER, and I mean NEVER have to say to anyone again, 'the man I love, I don't know where he is'.

Alex replied "Okay".

Then, as I slid my hands down the silk sleeves on his arms and took hold of his hands I said to him,

"Do you know what Alex, the best part of writing my book was, that I got the chance, to fall in love with you, all over again".

Then a bachata song came on and I said to him, "Do you want to dance to this?"

He replied "Absolutely".

Alex walked with me onto the dance floor and we got into the closed position hip to hip and really enjoyed moving to the very intimate music together. My hands were sliding all over his back, and the feel of the silk was so soft and sensuous. I said to Alex,

"A few months ago, I was talking to some friends about our relationship and I said that the only problem with the silk shirt was that I wouldn't be able to take it off you".

Alex replied, "Don't worry, I'll help you take it off".

It was just at that moment that our lips joined for the first time. Then when the song ended, Alex said to me, "Do you want to get out of here?"

I replied, "Absolutely".